Sandra Polley's
Knitted Toys

Sandra Polley's
Knitted Toys

Animals, dolls and teddies for all ages

COLLINS & BROWN

Published in the United Kingdom in 2016 by
Collins & Brown
1 Gower Street
London
WC1E 6HD

An imprint of Pavilion Books Company Ltd

Photography by Susan Crawford
Illustrations by Gavin Crawford

ISBN 978-1-91023-160-9

A CIP catalogue record for this book is available from
the British Library.

10 9 8 7 6 5 4 3 2 1

Reproduction by Colour Depth, UK
Printed and bound by Toppan Leefung Printing Ltd, China

This book can be ordered direct from the publisher at
www.pavilionbooks.com

Contents

Introduction

I hope if you are reading this it is because you love knitting and especially knitted toys. Being a bit lazy, I like a hobby that I can do sitting on my sofa. I might spread out a bit but when I've had enough it only takes a few minutes to put it all in a little bag. That's the great thing about knitting toys: it's relaxing, there's not much mess, it doesn't take too long, and hopefully there's something at the end of it that someone will actually want.

I have always loved craftwork, especially toy making. There is a feeling of creating a life, a little character, from just scraps of yarn or fabric, which if loved by a child will be given a name and a personality, perhaps even quite a long life.

So I have enjoyed making all of these different characters. Some were easier than others to design – it was difficult deciding how far to go with the glove puppets, and I thought I would never get the meerkat pattern finished. As with many people, though, I adore meerkats and just had to make one. I didn't want to give them the indignity of too many clothes, so they have only what they can

find on their travels around the desert. I hope they will appeal to both adults and children. They can be made smaller than the two sizes given by adjusting yarn and knitting needles – for example, I once made some very small ones as gifts for adult meerkat lovers using 3ply yarn and 2mm needles.

The idea for the glove puppets was a combination of my love of animals and wanting to make something for interactive play with my grandson Jack. The puppets can pick things up with their hands, including their own miniature baby. Each baby has a sleeping bag or blanket, so that the adult puppet can put the baby to bed.

Before you begin to knit any of the patterns, do take a few minutes to read the general instructions. Much of it you may already know, but it will help you to understand some of my peculiarities in toy making and also saves space by not having to repeat things for every pattern. All of the patterns are easy to follow, with no complicated stitches or designs, and many can be made from quite small amounts of yarn. The clothes have also

been kept to a simple design and are quick and easy to knit. The reindeer and elves are perfect for decorating a Christmas tree, and the miniature dolls and little bears such as Harriet and Brian can be quickly made for last-minute gifts or stocking fillers.

I hope you enjoy making these little characters and that they are loved by children young and old. I especially hope that you find knitting one relaxing, and that you like your finished toy and look forward to making another one.

Sandra Polley

Materials

Yarn

All of the yarn used to make the toys in this book was relatively cheap and is widely available, both in shops and online. So many places sell yarn and haberdashery items nowadays, not just specialist yarn shops – there is even a nice selection in my local chemist.

Yarn with a high wool content is not really suitable for these small toys, other than perhaps Jim and the baby's first teddy. The edges of the knitted pieces would curl in too much and make the projects, especially the small ones, difficult to sew up.

Knitting needles

There are not many different sizes of knitting needles used in this book. Most of the projects worked in DK yarn are knitted with 3mm needles. I have used the size needle I thought the most appropriate but, if you know that your knitting tension is usually too tight or too loose, you can use a size larger or smaller needles as appropriate.

If you are anything like me, you will have amassed a huge collection of needles over the years. The needle size conversion table will help you to identify the right size for your pattern.

Try to use shortish needles if you can – none of the knitted pieces has long rows, so long needles might get in the way.

Sewing needles

Needles for sewing knitted pieces together have a blunt point to prevent them from splitting the yarn and a large eye to thread the thick yarn through. They are generally called tapestry, yarn or knitters' needles and they are available in many different sizes. A medium size, either No. 18 or 20, is about right for sewing up DK and 4ply toys. You will also need a household sewing needle for sewing facial features, attaching press fasteners and a few other little bits.

Sewing thread

You will need some embroidery thread, mostly black or brown, for sewing noses. You could use yarn but it would be a bit thick for most of the toys.

You will also need a household sewing thread for attaching press fasteners and buttons, and some extra-strong black thread for sewing on bead eyes. I also use it for making mouse whiskers.

Stuffing

Years ago, teddy bears were stuffed with straw, wood, wool, kapok and so on, and during the war years, old bits of rags and clothes. Nowadays you can buy good-quality toy filling from haberdashers and craft shops. This stuffing is clean, light, relatively cheap and easy to use. It will also have been tested for fire resistance.

Another good source of stuffing can be found in new polyester quilts and pillows. You can buy inexpensive ones in many supermarkets and they will also have a safety standard mark, which means the stuffing will be fire resistant. Foam chips are no good for making small toys because they will make the toys lumpy as well as being difficult and messy to use.

Forceps or tweezers

These are very useful pieces of equipment and are essential when making Duncan, the miniature bear, and the glove puppet babies. They are used to help to turn the finished pieces the right way out after sewing up and also to grip and insert small amounts of stuffing into all the tiny spaces. Veterinary forceps are better than tweezers as they are slightly curved and have a locking ratchet. If you visit your local veterinary centre, they might be willing to order you a pair. Vetrerinary forceps are inexpensive and should last many years.

Pins

You should always use coloured plastic-headed pins for knitted toys as they can be easily seen and are not so likely to slip through and get lost in the knitting. Black-headed ones are very useful for trying out eye positions.

Stitch Holders

On some of the patterns you will need to put some stitches on a holder while knitting other pieces. A small safety pin is ideal for this or you can thread a length of differently coloured yarn onto a sewing up needle, thread it through the stitches to be held, knot and then pull it out when you have finished with it.

Scissors

A sharp pair of embroidery scissors are best to snip off threads. My favourites are the little plastic-handled, stainless steel ones you often see in supermarkets.

Tape measure

Although most of the instructions state the number of rows to knit, there are occasionally pieces of work to measure.

Pencil

A pencil is useful for marking where you are on the pattern as you go along or if you get disturbed. You can then erase the marks afterwards.

Eyes

Some of the eyes for these toys are embroidered. These are the safest eyes to use if the toy is for young children. Jim, Oscar and the glove puppets have plastic safety eyes. As the eyes I have used are a medium size, they are safe for older children because they are not small enough to slip out of the stitches and, if fixed in properly, they are almost impossible to pull out. Duncan, the miniature bear, and the meerkats have very small bead eyes. Bead eyes look very effective but must not be used for toys intended for babies and small children. Fred, Alice and a few teddy bears have looped-back eyes. You can buy loop backed eyes especially made for teddy bears from many craft retailer websites. They are flat backed, with a small loop moulded to the back so can be threaded into the head. They are not suitable for young children as they can be pulled out quite easily.

Buttons and beads

Many craft suppliers sell tiny buttons. Small beads also make nice buttons for miniature toys. I used gold beads for the elf and leprechaun jackets. Larger, household buttons make very good joints for toys for older children or adults. I like the quirky look of them on the outside of the limbs, as with the Christmas reindeer. There are a few projects in the book that require beads and sequins. Lots of pretty beads can be found in craft shops, car boot sales and charity shops. Sequins are sold in haberdashery shops and market places.

Safety

Most of the rules governing safety when making knitted toys for children are really just common sense.

• Scissors, needles and pins should not be left lying around when making the toy if there are young children about.

• Limbs must be sewn on securely.

• Any loose threads should be darned into the toys out of sight.

• Young children should not be given toys with tiny parts that can be pulled off and swallowed.

• Do not use beads, buttons or detachable eyes on toys or teddies intended for babies or children under 3 years of age, as they may cause a choking hazard if swallowed.

Note: You must remember to mention these safety rules if you make any of these toys for fundraising events.

General Instructions

How much yarn do I need?

For many of the patterns I have not stated how much yarn or stuffing you will need. For so many little toys, clothes and accessories, it would take forever to work it out and would not be very accurate either. A lot of it is down to common sense really. If a pattern states that you need embroidery thread for a miniature doll's eyes and you have more than a few centimetres, then you have plenty. You can usually look at an oddment of yarn and guess whether there is enough for a tiny doll's cardigan or meerkat's waistcoat. Having said that, I have tried to estimate the amount needed wherever I can.

Stitch patterns

Stocking stitch, garter stitch and single rib are the three main stitch patterns used in this book. A few others are used for clothes and these are explained in the project instructions.

STOCKING STITCH

All of the toys are knitted in stocking stitch. Duncan is sewn up with purl sides together, which when turned right way out becomes reverse stocking stitch.

GARTER STITCH

Some of the clothes and accessories are knitted in garter stitch, which means every row is knitted.

SINGLE RIB

All of the rib in this book is single rib, which is knit one, purl one to the end of the row, repeated across an even number of stitches.
For example:
Row 1: (K1, P1) twice.
Repeat this row until required length.

BRACKETS

When instructions are given in brackets, it means they are to be repeated the number of times stated.

Placing markers

Some of the patterns contain instructions to place markers.
For example:
Mark each end of last row.
This is to help with sewing up the pieces. A couple of the projects would be quite complicated to sew up without them. The easiest way to do this is to have a yarn needle threaded with a long length of yarn in a different shade from the one you are using for the knitting. Wherever you need to put a marker, make a couple

Needle sizes

mm	US	old UK
5	8	6
4.5	7	7
4	6	8
3.25	4	10
3	3	11
2.75	2	12
2.25	1	13

Abbreviations

alt	alternate
beg	beginning
cont	continue
dec	decrease by knitting/purling 2 stitches together
foll	following
g. st	garter stitch – every row knit
inc	increase by knitting/purling into front and back of a stitch
K	knit
m1	make 1 – make a stitch by lifting horizontal strand between last stitch worked and next stitch, place it on left-hand needle and knit into back of it
P	purl
rep	repeat
rib	K1, P1 across row
RS	right side of work
sl 1	slip next stitch
st(s)	stitch(es)
st st	stocking stitch – 1 row knit, 1 row purl
tog	together
WS	wrong side of work

of little stitches around the knitted stitch and then snip off close to the work. You can either carefully pull out the markers after completing all the sewing up or remove them as you get to them.

Increasing and decreasing

There are only two methods of increasing and decreasing used throughout the book. Some of the projects, such as waistcoats and some head gussets, need a smooth edge and so it is better to increase or decrease one stitch in from the edge. For example:
Decrease: K1, K2 tog, K to last 3 sts, K2 tog, K1.
or
Increase: K1, inc 1, K to last 2 sts, inc 1, K1.
However, you don't want any shaping to show on some of the seams, such as tiny doll faces or some of the clothes, so in those cases it is better to knit the two edge stitches together for decreasing or knit twice into the first and last stitch for increasing. Instructions for which method to use are given in the pattern.

Casting off

You will see that when casting off at the top of the limbs and in some other places, the instructions say either to slip the first stitch or knit two stitches together at each end of the row at the same time as casting off. This is to help smooth out the shaped edges of the seams and is quite easy to do. Cast off in the usual way but either slip the first stitch onto the right-hand needle without knitting it, or knit

2 together, cast off to the last 2 stitches, knit 2 together and cast off the last stitch.

Tension

Your tension is not too important for most of the toys because it does not really matter if your bear or toy comes out a little bit bigger or smaller than the finished size given. If you know that you are a very loose knitter then use a size smaller needles, or use larger needles if you knit tightly.

It is important, though, to use the same thickness of yarn for the clothes as used for the toy otherwise they might not fit. Some DK or 4ply yarns are thicker than others and this will also make a difference to the finished size.

Darning in yarn ends

Apart from the long yarn tail left at the top of Duncan the miniature bear's ears and maybe one or two other places, it is easier to use a yarn needle to darn all the loose threads into the edge or back of the work and trim them before sewing up. You might think that they are useful to sew up with but they only get in the way and are usually too short to use anyway.

Pressing

Not many of the knitted pieces need pressing. As most are sewn up with right sides together, the edges usually come together nicely. One exception is the miniature bear Duncan. His pieces will need a good press because they are to be sewn up with purl sides together to make a reverse stocking stitch bear. Pin the

pieces out, wrong side uppermost, on a flat pad or ironing board, cover them with a damp cloth and press with a warm iron.

Sewing up pieces

Always take your time sewing up the pieces and try to work in good light – daylight if possible. If you do work in the evening and need extra light, there are some very good halogen lamps available.

We all have our own way of doing things – for example, I always knot the end of any thread that I am sewing up with – and that is fine as long as the pieces are sewn together securely.

PINNING PIECES TOGETHER

When pinning small pieces of work together, insert the pins at right angles to the seam. This takes up less room and keeps the sharp point of the pins out of the way.

BACKSTITCH

This is a good stitch to use when you need a strong neat line or seam, such as the inside edge of Harriet bear's day bed.

Backstitch.

RUNNING STITCH

This is not used often for seaming because it is not very strong. It is useful as a tacking stitch for temporarily holding pieces in place before sewing more securely.

Running stitch.

OVERSEW STITCH

This stitch is very easy and is the best way to sew up all the little clothes. It is worked on the wrong side, with the right sides of the pieces held together. Take very small stitches from both edges of the work, one from each row, and work from back to front and then over to the back again for each stitch.

Oversew stitch.

LADDER STITCH

This is the best way to close a seam on the right side of the toy after stuffing it. Knot a length of thread and secure it at the edge of the opening in the seam.

Ladder stitch.

Take small stitches either side of the open seam, gently pulling the seam closed after every three or four stitches to the end. Secure with a couple more stitches.

Stuffing

As with all soft toys, how you stuff them will directly affect the finished appearance. It is important to stuff firmly but without stretching the knitting out of place. Always stuff well down into the extremities such as the nose and paws or hands first and mould into shape as you go along. A pair of forceps or tweezers is very useful for stuffing the smaller toys, especially the miniatures. If you are thread-jointing a finished bear, put plenty of stuffing in the body because the jointing will pull it in. The amount of stuffing needed for each toy will vary depending on knitting tension and individual taste.

Sewing faces

It is best to embroider facial features with embroidery thread rather than yarn, which is usually too thick.

For the little teddies in this book, a small neat triangle or rectangle sewn horizontally makes a good nose.

For the miniature dolls, 'less is more' so to speak. Use only one or two strands of embroidery thread at a time for the eyes (usually brown rather than black). Black-headed pins are ideal for trying out eye positions for all the toys. Make one tiny stitch and then sew two or three more exactly on top. Add a couple of tiny stitches on each eye to make eyelashes if you wish.

Although the mouth itself is only two or three stitches, how you place it will have a big impact on your toy's face and you may have to experiment a bit before you get the look you want. For the nose you could either sew two tiny stitches in brown or draw a couple of dots with a brown felt-tip pen.

Miniature doll face
Keep the features very small, with one tiny stitch sewn over and over a few times for the eyes.

The diagram below illustrates how eye position can determine your toy's personality.

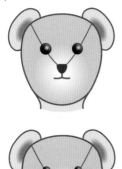

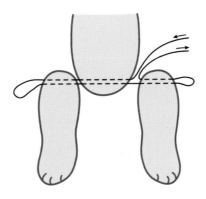

Teddy bear eyes
How you space the eyes on a bear can make him look younger or older, relaxed or puzzled.

Aftercare
Most of the toys can be washed by hand and spun inside a pillowcase. The larger ones will probably need to be dried outside on a warm day to make sure they are dry right through.

Thread-jointing
Use this technique to give jointed limbs for a poseable toy or teddy. First pin the limbs to the body. Check that the toy or teddy can sit or crouch correctly. Remove the limbs for now, replacing the pins in the exact position where the 'joints' are going to be. To attach each pair of limbs, thread a tapestry needle with a long piece of yarn and double it up. Starting at the first pin position and leaving a long thread, push the needle right through the body and out through the corresponding pin position on the other side. Take the needle right through one limb, then go back into the limb through exactly the same hole you came out of, but come out of the inside of the limb a couple of stitches away from where you went in. Go back through the body, then right through the second limb and back again, bringing needle out between the limb and the body (where you started). Pull the threads tightly, knot, then rethread and sink the ends into the body out of sight.

Thread-joint the limbs.

Workshop patterns

Quite often just a few variations in colour, yarn and needle size can produce completely different-looking toys. One example is how with a change of colour, longer legs and a set of antlers, Milly the little white dog became a Christmas reindeer. There are half a dozen or so toys throughout this book that have been adapted from the one before it. I call these 'workshop' patterns and they are clearly identified throughout the book. Just look for the ball of yarn logo, shown above, alongside the knitting pattern. After making a few toys you will probably see all sorts of variations to make your toys unique.

Toys

Hannah and Grace

Hannah wears a traditional long-sleeved dress, while Grace likes her up-to-date pink and white outfit. Both dolls and clothes are quickly knitted in stocking stitch.

HEIGHT
Approximately 30cm (12in)

MATERIALS
- 1 x 50g ball DK yarn in each of flesh pink (for Hannah) and brown (for Grace)
- 1 x 25g ball DK yarn in each of black (for Grace's hair and shoes) and yellow (for Hannah's hair)
- 1 x 50g ball DK yarn in light blue or pink for dress
- Oddments of DK yarn in white, pink and dark red for rest of clothes
- Length of medium blue yarn or embroidery thread for Hannah's eyes
- Pair each of 3mm and 3.25mm knitting needles
- Black, brown and white sewing thread
- Tapestry/yarn needle and small sewing needle
- Polyester stuffing
- 6 small press fasteners for dress and jumper
- 4 small white beads for decorating dress and jumper
- Thin pink ribbon for hair

Dolls

Both dolls are the same. Start all pieces with a K row unless otherwise stated.

Head and body
With 3mm needles and body colour of choice, cast on 37 sts.
Row 1: K2, (inc 1, K3) to last 3 sts, inc 1, K2 (46 sts).
St st 9 rows, ending on a P row.

TO SHAPE BOTTOM
Dec 1 st at each end of next and 3 foll alt rows (38 sts).
St st 19 rows, ending on a P row.

TO SHAPE SHOULDERS
Next row: K8, K2 tog twice, K14, K2 tog twice, K8 (34 sts).
Next row: P.
Next row: K7, K2 tog twice, K12, K2 tog twice, K7 (30 sts).
Next row: P.
Next row: K6, K2 tog twice, K10, K2 tog twice, K6 (26 sts).
St st 3 rows.

TO SHAPE HEAD
Next row: K2, inc 1, K2, inc in every st to last 5 sts, K2, inc 1, K2 (44 sts).

St st 9 rows, ending on a P row.
Next row: K10, K2 tog twice, K16, K2 tog twice, K10 (40 sts).
St st 13 rows, ending on a P row.
Next row: K2 tog across row (20 sts).
Next row: P2 tog across row (10 sts).
Break yarn, thread through remaining sts, pull up tight and fasten off, leaving a long thread to sew up head and body.

Arms – make 2
TO SHAPE HANDS
With 3mm needles and body colour, cast on 8 sts.
First row: Inc 1, K2, inc in next 2 sts, K2, inc 1 (12 sts).
Next row: P.
Inc 1 st at each end of next and foll alt row (16 sts).
Next row: P.
Dec 1 st at each end of next and foll alt row (12 sts).
St st 7 rows, ending on a P row.
Next row: Inc 1, K to last 2 sts, inc 1, K1 (14 sts).
St st 15 rows, ending on a P row.
Cast off, knitting 2 sts tog at each end of row at same time.

Legs – make 2
TO SHAPE FEET
With 3mm needles and white, cast on 9 sts.

First row: Inc in every st (18 sts).

Next row: P.

Next row: K1, inc in every st to last st, K1 (34 sts).

St st 3 rows.

Next row: K7, K2 tog 10 times, K7 (24 sts).

Next row: P.

Next row: K7, K2 tog 5 times, K7 (19 sts).

Next row: P.

Next row: K7, K2 tog 3 times, K6 (16 sts).

Next row: P7, P2 tog, P7 (15 sts).

Next row: K7, inc 1, K7 (16 sts).

St st 2 rows.

G. st 3 rows.

Change to body colour and starting with a K row, st st 10 rows.

Inc 1 st at each end of next and foll 10th row (20 sts).

St st 9 rows.

Cast off.

To make up
BODY AND HEAD
With RS together, fold lengthways and sew up seam from top of head to bottom cast on edge with appropriate coloured yarn, leaving a gap in doll's back for turning and stuffing. The seam lies at centre back of doll. Turn RS out and stuff head and shoulders carefully, filling out cheeks and moulding into shape as you go. Tie a length of body-coloured yarn

around neck, pull up tightly and fasten off. Stuff rest of body, pushing more stuffing into shoulders, but leave bottom few centimetres unstuffed. Tease out chin and cheeks with a yarn needle, digging quite deeply to pull the stuffing forwards.

EARS – OPTIONAL
The ears will not show much with long hair, so omit if you prefer. With body-coloured yarn and doll's face uppermost, take a pinch of knitting either side and about halfway up the head (on cheek shaping if you can see it) and backstitch about 2 or 3 sts through both layers down towards the neck. Secure with a couple more sts and fasten off.

LEGS
With RS together, fold each leg lengthways and sew up from bottom cast on edge to top. Turn RS out and stuff to within 1cm (½in) of top. Make sure stuffing is pushed well down into toes, moulding into shape as you go. With seam lying at centre back, press tops closed and oversew. Insert and sandwich top of legs just inside base of body, adjacent to the body sides and with a small gap between them. Backstitch through all layers. Finish stuffing body through gap in doll's back, pushing plenty of stuffing into bottom, and then close the seam.

ARMS
With RS together, fold each arm lengthways and sew up, leaving tops open. Turn RS out and stuff to within 2cm (¾in) of top. Flatten top of arms with seam lying at centre back. Oversew closed and sew top of arms to body under shoulder shaping.

FRINGE
Cut 20 lengths of hair-coloured yarn, about 15cm (6in) long, for the fringe. Lay them across top of head from front to back so that centre of bunch lies on crown. Backstitch in place. Place two pins on forehead, 5cm (2in) apart and 1cm (½in) down from crown. Pull all yarn strands forwards, fan them out and, with another length of yarn, backstitch fringe in place between pins. Trim fringe to about 4cm (1½in).

REST OF HAIR

Cut 60 lengths of hair-coloured yarn, about 30cm (12in) long. Working with 4 or 5 pieces at a time, backstitch centre of yarn lengths to seam line at back of head, starting 1cm (½in) up from neck and finishing just over fringe sewing line. To make sure that hair is spread out evenly, you could roughly tack into position first before sewing on neatly. You can add a few more lengths if there are any gaps but too many will make the finished hair bunches very thick. Gather each side of hair, tie into bunches and secure to head with 2 or 3 sts midway between top and bottom of head. Trim neatly and tie with ribbon.

HANNAH'S EYES

Take a length of blue yarn or embroidery thread and carefully split the strands apart. With 2 strands, darn the eyes to a round shape, just higher than halfway between chin and hairline and 2.5cm (1in) apart. Split a length of white yarn and, using 2 strands, backstitch a semicircle of 3 sts above and very close to each pupil (see diagram a).

Note: You do have to be careful splitting and then sewing with yarn because it becomes quite delicate and easily broken.

Diagram a.

HANNAH'S EYELASHES

With brown sewing thread, sew 2 tiny stitches outwards from each eye over the whites (see diagram b). With a double length of white sewing thread, sew a tiny stitch on each eye to bring them to life. Sew 2 little brown sts for eyebrows.

Diagram b.

GRACE'S EYES

Using black instead of blue yarn, sew eyes in a similar way as Hannah's but go over the whites a second time to round off and accentuate them a little more.

GRACE'S EYELASHES

With black sewing thread, sew 4 tiny sts outwards from pupil over the whites (see diagram c). Sew a tiny white stitch on each eye as for Hannah.

Diagram c.

MOUTH

Carefully split a length of red yarn and, with 2 strands, sew a mouth with 3 small sts halfway between eyes and chin.

NOSE – IF REQUIRED

Sew 2 tiny dots in pink slightly lower than midway between eyes and mouth.

Accessories
Knickers

Made in one piece, starting and finishing at waistband.

With 3.25mm needles and yarn colour of choice, cast on 21 sts and g. st 3 rows.

Next row: K2, (inc 1, K3) to last 3 sts, inc 1, K2 (26 sts).

Starting with a P row, st st 9 rows.

Next row: K1, K2 tog, K to last 3 sts, K2 tog, K1 (24 sts).

Next row: K1, P2 tog, P to last 3 sts, P2 tog, K1 (22 sts).

Rep last 2 rows until 6 sts remain, ending on a P row.

St st 2 rows.

Inc 1 st at each end of every row until 26 sts, ending on a P row.

St st 8 rows.

Next row: K2, (K2 tog, K3) to last 4 sts, K2 tog, K2 (21 sts).

G. st 3 rows.

Cast off.

With K sides tog, fold and sew up side seams.

Dress
SKIRT

With 3.25mm needles and blue or pink yarn, cast on 104 sts and work in K1, P1 rib for 2 rows.

Starting with a K row, st st 18 rows.

START OF BACK OPENING

Next row: Cast on 2 sts at beg of row.

Next row: K2, P to last 2 sts, K2.
Cont in st st for a further 10 rows,
keeping first and last 2 sts K in every row.
Next row: K3, K2 tog to last 3 sts, K3
(56 sts).
G. st 3 rows.

BODICE

Keeping g. st borders correct, st st 6 rows
straight, ending on a P row.

TO SHAPE LEFT BACK

Next row: K13, K2 tog, turn and work
on these 14 sts only for now.
Keeping g. st border correct, cont to
dec 1 st at inside armhole edge on next
3 rows (11 sts).
Work 9 rows straight, ending on a K row.

TO SHAPE SHOULDERS

Next row: Cast off 4 sts at beg of row,
work to end.
Cast off 2 sts, break yarn and leave
remaining 5 sts on a holder.

FRONT

With RS facing, rejoin yarn, K2 tog, K22,
K2 tog, turn and work on these 24 sts
only for now.
Dec 1 st at each end of next 3 rows
(18 sts).
St st 4 rows straight.

TO SHAPE NECK

K5, K2 tog, turn.
Next row: P2 tog, P to end.
Next row: K to last 2 sts, K2 tog (4 sts).
Work 3 rows straight.
Cast off.

With RS facing, leave next 4 sts on a
holder for centre front neck, then rejoin
yarn, K2 tog, K to end.
Complete to match left side of neck,
reversing shaping.

TO SHAPE RIGHT BACK

With RS facing, rejoin yarn to remaining
sts, K2 tog, K to end.
Keeping g. st border correct, dec 1 st at
armhole edge on next 3 rows (11 sts).
Work 10 rows straight, ending on a
P row.

TO SHAPE SHOULDERS

Next row: Cast off 4 sts at beg of row,
work to end.
Next row: Cast off 2 sts, P to end and
leave remaining 5 sts on a holder.
With RS together, join shoulder seams.

COLLAR

With 3mm needles, white yarn and RS
facing, K the 5 sts from left back holder,
pick up and K 8 sts down left neck edge
and 2 of the 4 sts from holder at front
neck (15 sts).
Turn and work on these sts only for now.
G. st 4 rows, finishing at centre front
neck.
Next row: K2 tog, K to end.
Next row: K.
Rep last 2 rows twice (12 sts).
Cast off, knitting 2 sts tog at beg of row.
With RS facing, rejoin yarn and K the
2 remaining sts from front neck holder,
pick up and K 8 sts along right neck edge
and K 5 sts of right back.
G. st 4 rows, finishing at back edge.

Next row: K to last 2 sts, K2 tog.
Next row: K.
Rep last 2 rows twice (12 sts).
Cast off, knitting 2 sts tog at end of row at
same time.
With WS facing, catch collar centre front
together with 1 or 2 sts to neaten. Darn in
and snip off loose ends.

LONG SLEEVES – MAKE 2

With 3mm needles and white yarn, cast
on 20 sts and g. st 2 rows.
Change to 3.25mm needles and blue or
pink yarn.
Starting with a K row, continued in st st
and inc 1 st at each end of next and foll
6th row (24 sts).
St st 7 rows straight, ending on a P row.
Mark each end of last row.

TO SHAPE TOP

Dec 1 st at each end of next 3 rows
(18 sts).
Next row: P.

Dec 1 st at each end of next and foll alt row (14 sts).
Cast off, purling 2 sts tog at each end of row at same time.
Join underarm seams from cast on edge to markers. With RS together, sew in sleeves. Sew up back seam of dress from hem to start of back opening. Overlap the g. st borders with the 2 cast on sts on inside and catch down with a couple of sts. Sew on 3 press fasteners, evenly spaced. Decorate front of dress with 2 beads or (for younger children) perhaps a couple of French knots.

Jumper
With 3mm needles and white yarn, cast on 56 sts.
Work in K1, P1 rib for 2 rows.
Change to 3.25mm needles.
Next row: K.
Next row: K2, P to last 2 sts, K2.
Rep last 2 rows 4 times.
Complete as for bodice of dress from start of left back shaping.

SHORT SLEEVES – MAKE 2
With 3mm needles and white yarn, cast on 20 sts and g. st 2 rows.
Change to 3.25mm needles.
Next row: (Inc 1, K5) to last 2 sts, inc 1, K1 (24 sts).
St st 3 rows, ending on a P row.
Mark each end of last row.
Shape tops as for long sleeves of dress.
Finish jumper in same way as dress, sewing press fasteners to back and adding a couple of beads or a length of yarn tied into a bow at front of collar.

Trousers – make 2 pieces
With 3.25mm needles and pink yarn, cast on 30 sts and g. st 2 rows.
Starting with a K row, st st 26 rows.
Mark each end of last row.

TO SHAPE CROTCH
Cast off 2 sts at beg of next 2 rows.
Next row: Dec 1 st at each end of row.
St st 15 rows.
Next row: K2, K2 tog, (K4, K2 tog) to last 2 sts, K2 (20 sts).
G. st 3 rows.
Cast off.

POCKETS – MAKE 2
With 3.25mm needles and pink yarn, cast on 9 sts.
Starting and ending with a K row, st st 9 rows.
K 1 row.
Cast off.

TO MAKE UP
With RS together, fold each leg lengthways and sew up each inside leg seam from bottom cast on edge to marker. Turn one leg RS out and fit into the other, matching crotch seams. Sew from front to back, leaving last 2cm (¾in) of seam open for back fastening. Sew press fastener onto waistband at this opening for easy dressing. Sew pockets in place either side of front seam.

Shoes – make 2
With 3mm needles and red or black yarn, cast on 9 sts and work in st st.
First row: Inc in every st (18 sts).

Next row: P.
Next row: Inc in every st (36 sts).
St st 3 rows.
Next row: K8, K2 tog 10 times, K8 (26 sts).
Next row: P.
Next row: K7, K2 tog 6 times, K7 (20 sts).
Next row: P.
Next row: K5, turn and P back, slipping first st.
Next row: K across all sts.
Next row: P5, turn and K back, slipping first st.
Cast off purlwise.
With RS together, fold shoe and sew up seam from underfoot to cast off edge at back of ankle. Turn RS out, press out and shape toe of shoes with finger and thumb. Sew a length of yarn under a stitch at centre front of shoe upper to form two equal-sized laces, tie a small bow and trim ends.

Meerkat Family

Apart from the head pieces being a bit fiddly to sew up, these little animals are not as complicated to make as they look. The back legs are knitted into the body to become all one piece. The top of the arms (which are one piece each) are knitted into a row, so only the head and tail are sewn on afterwards. If you mark the rows where stated, sewing up will then become much easier.

HEIGHT

Adult: approximately 24cm (9½in)
Junior: approximately 18cm (7in)

MATERIALS

- 1 x 50g ball DK yarn in sand colour for each adult meerkat and about ½ ball of same for each junior meerkat
- Oddments of DK yarn for accessories
- Pair of 3mm knitting needles
- Two 5mm beads for adult, eyes
- Two 4mm beads for junior, eyes
- Extra-strong black thread
- Medium brown embroidery thread for eye patches, nose and mouth
- Brown eyebrow pencil (optional)
- Black embroidery thread for claws
- Embellishments such as buttons for waistcoats and strings of beads for necklaces (optional)
- Tapestry/yarn needle and small sewing needle
- Polyester stuffing

Note: The meerkats can also be knitted in 4ply yarn using 2.75mm needles and 3mm beads for eyes.

Adult Meerkat

Left arm

Cast on 2 sts and work in st st.
Next row: Inc in each st (4 sts).
Next row: P.
Next row: Inc 1, K to last 2 sts, inc 1, K1.
St st 3 rows.
Inc as before at each end of next and foll alt row (10 sts).
Next row: P.
Next row: Inc 1, K2, K2 tog twice, K1, inc 1, K1.
Next row: P.
Rep last 2 rows twice.

TO SHAPE TOP OF ARM

Next row: K5, m1, K5.
Next row: P.
Next row: K5, m1, K1, m1, K5 (13 sts).
Next row: P.
Next row: K5, m1, K3, m1, K5 (15 sts).
Next row: P.
Next row: K5, m1, K5, m1, K5 (17 sts).*
Next row: Cast off 7 sts, P to end (10 sts). Mark each end of last row.
St st 2 rows.
Leave sts on a holder.

Right arm

Work as for left arm to *.
Next row: P10, cast off last 7 sts (10 sts).
Break yarn and mark each end of last row.
Rejoin yarn and st st 2 rows.
Leave sts on a holder.

Body, legs and feet

Cast on 4 sts and work in st st.
Next row: Inc in each st (8 sts).
Next row: P.
Next row: K1, inc in every st to last st, K1 (14 sts).
Next row: P.
Next row: K5, K2 tog twice, K5 (12 sts).
Next row: P.
Next row: K4, K2 tog twice, K4 (10 sts).
Next row: P.
Next row: Inc 1, K2, K2 tog twice, K2, inc 1.
Next row: P.
Rep last 2 rows once.
Next row: K4, K2 tog, K4.
Next row: P.
Next row: K2 tog, K2, m1, K1, m1, K2, K2 tog.

Next row: P.
Mark each end of last row.
Leave these sts on a holder and make another foot the same.
Next row: Cast on 5 sts at beg of row, K until there are 8 sts on right needle, m1, K3, m1, K to end, turn and cast on 6 sts, turn back and K across first 3 sts of other foot, m1, K3, m1, K to end, turn and cast on 5 sts (38 sts).
Mark each end of last row.
Next row: P.
Next row: Inc 1, K7, m1, K5, m1, K4, K2 tog twice, K4, m1, K5, m1, K6, inc 1, K1 (42 sts).
Next row: P.

TO SHAPE BOTTOM
Next row: K7, turn, sl 1, P back.

K6, turn, sl 1, P back.
K5, turn, sl 1, P back.
Next row: K9, m1, K7, m1, K3, K2 tog twice, K3, m1, K7, m1, K9 (44 sts).
Next row: P7, turn, sl 1, K back.
P6, turn, sl 1, K back.
P5, turn, sl 1, K back.
Next and every foll alt row: P.
Next K row: (K9, m1) twice, K2, K2 tog twice, K2, (m1, K9) twice (46 sts).
Next K row: K9, m1, K11, m1, K1, K2 tog twice, K1, m1, K11, m1, K9 (48 sts).
Next K row: K9, m1, K13, m1, K4, m1, K13, m1, K to end (52 sts).
Next K row: K9, m1, K15, m1, K4, m1, K15, m1, K9 (56 sts).
St st 3 rows.
Next K row: K28, m1, K28.
Next K row: K28, m1, K1, m1, K28 (59 sts).

TO SHAPE KNEES
Next K row: K16, K2 tog twice, K19, K2 tog twice, K to end.
Next K row: K14, cast off next 7 sts, K until there are 14 sts on right needle for centre section, cast off next 7 sts, K to end (41 sts).
Next P row: P to end, pulling sts tog tightly at cast off sections to shape knees (gaps will be sewn closed later).
St st 20 rows straight, ending on a P row.
Next row: K5, (K2 tog, K4) to end (35 sts).

TO JOIN ARMS
Next row: P7, cast off next 7 sts, P7, cast off next 7 sts, P7.

Next row: K7, K across sts of left arm, K7, K across sts of right arm, K7 (41 sts).
St st 7 rows, ending on a P row.
Next row: K10, K2 tog twice, K until 14 sts remain, K2 tog twice, K to end (37 sts).
Next row: P.
Next row: K1, K2 tog to end (19 sts).
Cast off.

Head
LEFT SIDE
Cast on 7 sts.
Starting with a K row, st st 2 rows.
Next row: K3, K2 tog, K2.
St st 2 rows.
Next row: Cast on 8 sts, P11, m1, P to end (15 sts).
Next row: K to last 2 sts, K2 tog.
Next row: P2 tog, P to end.
Rep last 2 rows until 9 sts remain.
St st 2 rows.
Cont to dec 1 st at nose end on next 2 rows (7 sts).
Cast off, knitting 2 sts tog at each end of row at same time.

RIGHT SIDE
Work as for left side, starting with a P row and reversing shaping by reading K for P and P for K.

HEAD GUSSET
Cast on 6 sts.
Starting with a K row, st st 24 rows.
Dec 1 st at each end of next and foll 4th row.
P 1 row.
K2 tog and fasten off.

Tail

Cast on 4 sts.

P 1 row.

Next row: Inc 1, K1, inc 1, K1 (6 sts).

St st 7 rows.

Cont to inc 1 st at each end of every 8th row until there are 16 sts.

St st 3 rows.

Cast off.

Allow tail to roll in naturally and then tighten the roll a bit more. Slip stitch the underseam up to top. About halfway along, anchor thread with an extra stitch, continue sewing up for about 2cm (¾in), pull yarn gently to curve tail, anchor with another stitch and then finish sewing up.

To make up

Sew up all pieces using a tiny oversew stitch unless otherwise stated.

BODY

With K sides together, fold feet lengthways and sew seam up to markers. Join back seam to about halfway up back, matching bottom markers. To finish sewing the bottom, flatten out body so that lower back seam is at centre and sew up horizontal seam that has formed between feet (see diagram, right). Fold cast off edges of knees in half and oversew closed, deep enough to prevent cast off stitches from showing on RS. Turn RS out. Fold arms RS together and sew seams up to markers. Turn RS out and, from inside of body, sew cast off edge of arms to cast off edge of body. You really need forceps or tweezers to turn the limbs RS out as they are a bit fiddly.

Stuff body, but push only tiniest bit of stuffing into toes and do not stuff 'ankles'. Push plenty of stuffing into bottom, shaping with your hands at the same time. Ladder stitch rest of body closed and then stuff rest of back. The shoulders need to be shaped with plenty of stuffing but only push a tiny bit of stuffing into tops of arms. You will see as you work how they will hang as you stuff and shape the shoulders.

HEAD

With RS together for all sewing up, first join chin seam up to tip of nose. Pin and sew in head gusset. Try to sew edges of gusset to inside of cast off sts at top of head so that they do not show. Turn RS out and stuff carefully, pushing stuffing well down into nose first and moulding head into shape. Do not worry at this point that the head is not the correct shape yet: inserting the eyes will pull it into the correct shape. Sew head to body, adding extra stuffing as you go to keep the neck firm.

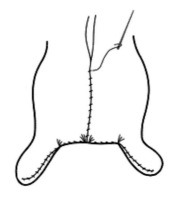

To hold arms to body, either sew tip of paws together with a couple of sts or knot a length of yarn, take it through into back and come out just below elbow position. Take a couple of sts of the arm, go through body to other side and repeat. Pull gently, just enough to keep arms close to sides, and fasten off, sinking ends into body out of sight.

EARS

Thread a length of brown yarn onto a needle, double it up and knot the end. Go into head through back of neck and come out at side and towards back of head. Make 3 sts about 1cm (½in) long over top of each other, keeping them loose enough to build up the ear. Take needle through head to second ear position (do not pull thread tightly) and repeat.

EYES AND HEAD SHAPING

Mark eye positions with two pins (halfway along gusset line between nose tip and top of head). With 2 strands of medium brown embroidery thread, darn an eye shape along seam line around each pin, building up to quite a round shape. It will be easier if you turn the head over to one side to do each eye (see diagrams overleaf). If you think the eye 'patches' need to be a bit larger, a brown eyebrow pencil applied around outside of sts is very effective. You could find some photographs of meerkats as reference. Remove pins and insert beads in same way as for Duncan bear (see page 84).

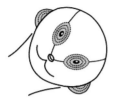

Using 5mm beads for the adult. Pull eyes in quite firmly and they will flatten and shape the head. When you are happy with the shape, secure threads well at back of neck and then sink them into body out of sight. With 3 strands of brown embroidery thread, sew 3 little stitches for nose and 2 long stitches for mouth (refer to photographs).

TAIL

Sit the meerkat and hold top of tail against bottom in a satisfactory position (seam at underside) so that the meerkat can sit comfortably. Pin if necessary or tack with a couple of sts of contrasting coloured yarn. Starting at top, oversew tail to body about three-quarters of the way around. For the adult, add a very small amount of stuffing inside top of tail and then finish sewing on.

Junior Meerkat

Left arm

Cast on 2 sts and work in st st.

First row: Inc in each st (4 sts).

Next row: P.

Next row: Inc 1, K1, inc 1, K1 (6 sts).
St st 3 rows.

Next row: Inc 1, K3, inc 1, K1 (8 sts).

Next row: P.

Next row: Inc 1, K1, K2 tog twice, inc 1, K1.

Next row: P.
Rep last 2 rows twice.
St st 2 rows.

TO SHAPE TOP OF ARM

Next row: K4, m1, K4 (9 sts).

Next row: P.

Next row: K4, m1, K1, m1, K4 (11 sts).

Next row: P.

Next row: K4, m1, K3, m1, K4 (13 sts).**

Next row: Cast off 5 sts, P to end.
St st 2 rows. Leave sts on a holder.

Right arm

Work as for first arm to **.

Next row: P to last 5 sts, cast off 5 sts.
Rejoin yarn and st st 2 rows.
Leave sts on a holder.

Body, legs and feet

Starting at feet, cast on 6 sts and work in st st.

Row 1: Inc in each st (12 sts).

Row 2: P.

Row 3: K2 tog, K2, K2 tog twice, K2, K2 tog (8 sts).

Row 4: P.

Row 5: Inc 1, K1, K2 tog twice, inc 1, K1.

Row 6: P.

Row 7: Rep row 5.

Row 8: P3, P2 tog, P3.

Row 9: K3, m1, K1, m1, K3 (9 sts).

Row 10: P.
Mark each end of last row and leave these sts on a holder.
Make a second foot exactly the same, then:

Next row: Cast on 4 sts, K until there are 7 sts on right-hand needle, m1, K3, m1, K3, turn, cast on 4 sts, turn back and K across first 3 sts of first foot, m1, K3, m1, K to end, turn and cast on 4 sts (34 sts).

Next row: P.
Mark each end of last row. This marking is quite important for matching seams and sewing up later.

Next row: K7, m1, K5, m1, K3, K2 tog twice, K3, m1, K5, m1, K 7 (36 sts).

Next row: P.

TO SHAPE BOTTOM

Next row: K6, turn, sl 1, P back.
K5, turn, sl 1, P back.
K4, turn, sl 1, P back.
K3, turn, sl 1, P back.

Next row: K7, m1, K7, m1, K2, K2 tog twice, K2, m1, K7, m1, K 7.

Next row: P6, turn, sl 1, K back.
P5, turn, sl 1, K back.
P4, turn, sl 1, K back.

P3, turn, sl 1, K back.
Next row: P.
Next row: K7, m1, K9, m1, K1, K2 tog twice, K1, m1, K9, m1, K7 (40 sts).
Next row: P.
Next row: K7, m1, K11, m1, K2 tog twice, m1, K11, m1, K7.
Next row: P.
Next row: K20, m1, K1, m1, K21.
Next row: P.
Next row: K20, m1, K3, m1, K21 (46 sts).
St st 3 rows.

TO SHAPE KNEES
Next row: K10, cast off next 7 sts, K until 17 sts remain on left-hand needle, cast off next 7 sts, K to end (32 sts).
Next row: P to end, pulling sts together tightly at each end of cast off sts to form knees (gap will be sewn closed later).
St st 4 rows straight.

TO SHAPE BACK
Next row: K2 tog, K to last 3 sts, turn, sl 1, P to last 3 sts, turn, sl 1, K to end.
Next row: P2 tog, P to end (30 sts).
St st 6 rows straight.
Next row: K8, K2 tog, K to last 10 sts, K2 tog, K to end (28 sts).

TO INSERT ARMS
Next row: P6, cast off next 5 sts, P until there are 6 sts on right-hand needle for chest, cast off next 5 sts, P to end.
You should now have three sets of 6 sts.
Next row: K6, K across sts of left arm, K6, K across sts of right arm, K to end (34 sts).

St st 3 rows.
Next row: K8, K2 tog twice, K until 12 sts remain, K2 tog twice, K to end (30 sts).
Next row: P.
Next row: K2 tog to end (15 sts).
Next row: P.
Cast off.

Tail
Starting at tip, cast on 3 sts.
Starting with a K row, st st 6 rows.
Next row: Inc in first and last st (5 sts).
St st 7 rows.
Cont to inc 1 st in next and every 4th row until 15 sts.
St st 3 rows.
Cast off.
Sew up tail as for Adult Meerkat.

Head
Starting at neck, cast on 12 sts.
Starting with a P row, st st 3 rows.

LEFT SIDE
K6, turn and work on these sts only for now.
Next row: Cast on 7 sts at beg of row, P these sts and to end of row (13 sts).
Next row: K to last 2 sts, K2 tog.
Next row: P2 tog, P to end.
Cont to dec like this at nose end until 7 sts remain.
Cast off, knitting 2 sts tog at each end of row at same time.

RIGHT SIDE
With RS facing, rejoin yarn.
Next row: K.

Next row: P.
Next row: Cast on 7 sts at beg of row, K these sts and to end of row (13 sts).
Next row: P to last 2 sts, P2 tog.
Next row: K1, K2 tog, K to end.
Cont to dec like this until 7 sts remain.
Cast off purlwise as first side.

HEAD GUSSET
Starting at nose, cast on 2 sts.
Next row: Inc 1, K1.
Next row: P.
Next row: Inc 1, K2 (4 sts).
St st 3 rows.
Next row: Inc 1, K to last 2 sts, inc 1, K1.
Next row: P.
Rep last 2 rows (8 sts).
St st 8 rows straight.
Next row: K1, K2 tog, K to last 3 sts, K2 tog, K1.
St st 7 rows.
Cast off.

To make up
Sew up and complete in same way as Adult Meerkat, using 4mm beads for the eyes.

Accessories
Adult waistcoat
Worked in g. st throughout.
With 3mm needles, cast on 36 sts and K 1 row.
Inc 1 st at each end of next and foll alt row (40 sts).
K 4 rows straight.

DIVIDE FOR FRONT AND BACK

Next row: K6, cast off next 6 sts, K until there are 16 sts on needle for back, cast off next 6 sts, K6.

FIRST SIDE

Next row: K.
Next row: K2 tog, K to end.
K 8 rows straight, ending at front edge.
Next row: K1, K2 tog, K to end.
K 5 rows, ending at front edge.
Rep last 6 rows.
Cast off remaining 3 sts.

BACK

With RS facing, rejoin yarn to next 16 sts, K2 tog at each end of row.
K 18 rows straight.
Cast off.

SECOND SIDE

Rejoin yarn at inside armhole edge and K to end.
Next row: K to last 2 sts, K2 tog.
K 8 rows straight, ending at armhole edge.
Next row: K to last 3 sts, K2 tog, K1.
K 5 rows straight.
Rep last 6 rows.
Cast off.
Sew up shoulder seams.
If required, with contrast yarn, blanket stitch all around outer edges. Sew on buttons if you wish

Collar

For a simple collar, wrap a length of brightly coloured yarn around the neck two or three times, knot at the front and trim.

Lace Collar

For Mummy Meerkat's lace collar make eyelet hole in row 1, yarn over twice, bring yarn to front of work then wrap round needle once more anticlockwise. This will make 2 extra sts.
With 2¾ mm needles cast on 5 sts.
Row 1: Sl 1, K2, yarn over twice, K2 (7 sts).
Row 2: Sl 1, P2, K4.
Row 3: Sl 1, K6.
Row 4: Cast off 2 sts, P1, K3 (5 sts).
Repeat last 4 rows until collar fits nicely around Mummy's neck.
Cast off.
Join at the front with a couple of sts, and perhaps a small bead for a 'brooch'.

Scarf

With yellow yarn, cast on 4 sts.
G. st 8 rows each of yellow, green, blue and light brown (3 times each).
Cast off and fringe as for Jim bear's scarf (see page 77).

Junior waistcoat

Worked in g. st throughout.
With 3mm needles, cast on 34 sts.
Inc 1 st at each end of next and foll alt row (38 sts).
K 7 rows straight.

TO SHAPE RIGHT SIDE

Next row: K9, turn and work on these sts only for now.
Next row: Cast off 3 sts, K to end.
Next row: K.
Next row: Dec 1 st at beg of row.
K 2 rows.

TO SHAPE FRONT

Next row: K1, K2 tog, K to end.
K 3 rows.
Next row: K1, K2 tog, K1.
K 6 rows.
Cast off.

TO SHAPE BACK

Rejoin yarn at inside (armhole) edge.
Next row: Cast off 3 sts, K until there are 17 sts on right-hand needle, turn and work on these sts only for now.

TO SHAPE ARMHOLE

Next row: Cast off 3 sts, K to end.
Next row: Dec 1 st at each end of row (12 sts).
Work straight for 10 rows.
Cast off.

TO SHAPE LEFT SIDE

Starting at armhole edge, rejoin yarn to remaining 9 sts.
Next row: Cast off 3 sts, K to end.
Next row: K.
Next row: Dec 1 st at beg of row.
K 2 rows.
Complete as for right side from beginning of front shaping.
Make up as for adult waistcoat, adding buttons or beads if required.

Junior backpack

With 3mm needles and DK yarn, work as for the Miniature Dolls' backpack (see page 65). Use 2.75mm needles for the straps. Each strap should measure 9cm (3½in) long, unstretched.

Naughty Little Rats

To knit one of these naughty little rats, follow the instructions for Junior Meerkat (see page 26) with the few simple adaptations explained below.

HEIGHT
Approximately 20cm (7¾in)

MATERIALS
- 1 x 25g or 50g ball of DK yarn in white or dark grey
- Oddments of DK yarn in pink for paws, ears and tail, plus yellow or blue for jumper
- Pair each of 3mm and 3.25mm knitting needles
- Two 4mm beads for eyes
- Extra-strong thread for whiskers
- Tapestry/yarn needle
- Polyester stuffing

Rats

Arms
With 3mm needles and pink yarn, work as for Junior Meerkat until there are 6 sts, ending on a P row.
St st 2 rows.
Change to 3.25mm needles and blue or yellow yarn.
Next row: Inc 1, K3, inc 1, K1 (8 sts).
Next row: K.
Next row: Inc 1, K1, K2 tog twice, inc 1, K1.
Next row: P.
Rep last 2 rows.
Complete as for Junior Meerkat from beginning of top of arm shaping.

Body, legs and feet
Starting at feet, using 3mm needles and pink yarn, work as for Junior Meerkat but omit rows 6 and 7.
Change to white or grey yarn on row 9.
Cont as for Junior Meerkat to end of knee shaping.
Leave sts on a spare needle.

JUMPER

With 3mm needles and blue or yellow yarn, cast on 36 sts and rib 3 rows.
Next row: Rib 5, (K2 tog, rib 6) 3 times, K2 tog, rib 5 (32 sts).
Next row: Hold spare needle with body sts adjacent to and behind needle with rib sts.
With 3.25mm needle, K 1 st from each needle together to end (32 sts).
P 1 row.
With 3.25mm needles, complete as for Junior Meerkat body from beginning of back shaping to last two rows.
Next row: K2, (K2 tog) to last 2 sts, K2.
Next row: P.
Cast off.

Head

With 3mm needles and white or grey yarn, cast on 12 sts and P 1 row.
Next row: K6, turn, cast on 8 sts, P across these sts and to end of row (14 sts).
Next row: K to last 2 sts, K2 tog.
Next row: P2 tog, P to end.
Cont to dec 1 st at nose end on every row until 7 sts remain.
P 1 row.
Cast off.
With K side facing, rejoin yarn, cast on 8 sts and K to end.
Dec 1 st at nose end on every row as for first side, reversing shaping.
K 1 row.
Cast off.

HEAD GUSSET

As for Junior Meerkat (see page 28).

Ears – make 2

With 3mm needles and pink yarn, cast on 5 sts and K 2 rows.
Next row: Inc 1, K1, K to last 2 sts, inc 1, K1.
K 4 rows.
Next row: K1, K2 tog, K to last 3 sts, K2 tog, K1.
Cast off, leaving a longish thread.

To make up

Make up the rats as for the meerkats but sew back seam of jumper welt separately from body. Sew ears on upside down (cast off sts to head), well back on head and with sides curled inwards. Sew 3 or 4 pink sts for nose. When inserting eyes, do not pull tightly as for the meerkats because you do not want a flattened face. Attach whiskers as for Fred and Alice mice (see page 35).
For fluff between ears, thread a length of yarn onto a tapestry yarn needle, double it up and knot the end. Take needle in through back of neck and come out at top of head. Pull yarn through and trim to about 2cm (¾in). Repeat a couple of times. Fluff up threads with end of needle.

COLLAR

With 3mm needles and blue or yellow yarn, cast on 26 sts and rib 7 rows.
Cast off in rib.
Wrap around and sew bottom edge to neck. Sew up seam at back and fold over.

TAIL

With 3mm needles and pink yarn, cast on 3 sts and work in st st for 6 rows.
Inc 1 st at each end of next and every 8th row until 11 sts. St st 7 rows. Cast off.
Sew on tail as for meerkats.

Fred and Alice

These quirky little mice would be perfect as gifts peeping out of the top of a Christmas stocking. They are very easy to make but their limbs are a bit fiddly to stuff. A pair of forceps is ideal for this job but eyebrow tweezers can also be used.

HEIGHT
Approximately 23cm (9in) to top of ears

MATERIALS
- 1 x 50g ball 4ply yarn in mousy colour (sufficient for both mice)
- Oddments of 4ply yarn in red and cream for skirt and scarf
- Pair of 2.75mm knitting needles
- Tapestry/yarn needle
- Forceps or tweezers for turning and stuffing
- Polyester stuffing
- Two 4mm black beads for eyes or black embroidery thread
- Extra-strong black thread for whiskers
- Dark brown embroidery thread for mouth and claws
- Very small amount of medium brown yarn for nose or brown felt-tip pen
- String of beads for necklace

Mice

Body
Cast on 28 sts.
Row 1: K13, inc in next 2 sts, K13.
Row 2 and every foll alt row: P.
Row 3: K14, inc in next 2 sts, K14.
Row 5: K15, inc in next 2 sts, K15.
Row 7: K16, inc in next 2 sts, K16.
Row 9: K17, inc in next 2 sts, K17 (38 sts).
St st 15 rows straight.
Next row: K17, K2 tog twice, K17.
Next row: P.
Next row: K16, K2 tog twice, K16.
Next row: P.
Next row: K15, K2 tog twice, K15 (32 sts).
Next row: P.

TO SHAPE SHOULDERS
Next row: *K5, K2 tog twice, rep from * twice, K5 (26 sts).
Next row: P.
Next row: K4, K2 tog twice, *K3, K2 tog twice, rep from * once, K4 (20 sts).
Next row: P.
Cast off.
Place marker at each end of last row

about 1cm (½in) up from cast on edge. This will be for tail placement later on.

Head
SIDE A
Cast on 8 sts and starting with a K row, st st 4 rows.
Next row: K to last 2 sts, inc 1, K1.
Next row: Cast on 10 sts, P these sts and to end of row (19 sts).
Next row: K to last 2 sts, K2 tog.
Next row: P2 tog, P to end.
Cont to dec 1 st at nose end on every row until 8 sts remain.
Next row: Dec 1 st at each end of row. Cast off, knitting 2 sts tog at each end of row at same time.

SIDE B
Cast on 8 sts and starting with a P row, st st 4 rows.
Next row: P to last 2 sts, inc 1, P1.
Next row: Cast on 10 sts, K these sts and to end of row (19 sts).
Next row: P to last 2 sts, P2 tog.
Next row: K2 tog, K to end.
Complete to match side A, reversing shaping.

HEAD GUSSET

Cast on 2 sts, leaving a long thread to identify nose end.

Starting with a K row, work in st st.

First row: Inc in each st (4 sts).

Next row: P.

Next row: Inc 1 st at each end of row (6 sts).

Cont straight in st st until work measures 9cm (3½in), ending on a P row.

Next row: Dec 1 st at each end of row.

Cont straight until work measures 11cm (4¼in), ending on a P row.

Cast off.

Ears – make 4 pieces

Starting at top of ear, cast on 8 sts.

Starting with a K row, st st 2 rows.

Next row: Inc 1, K to last 2 sts, inc 1, K1 (10 sts).

St st 4 rows.

Next row: Dec 1 st at each end of row (8 sts).

Cast off, knitting 2 sts tog at each end of row at same time.

Legs – make 2

Starting at feet, cast on 23 sts.

Starting with a K row, work in st st.

First row: Inc 1 st at each end of row (25 sts).

St st 4 rows.

Next row: Dec 1 st at each end of row (23 sts).

Cast off 6 sts at beg of next 2 rows (11 sts).

Cont in st st until work measures 10cm (4 in).

Cast off.

Arms – make 2

Starting at paws, cast on 6 sts.

Row 1: K2, inc in next 2 sts, K2.

Row 2 and every foll alt row: P.

Row 3: K3, inc in next 2 sts, K3.

Row 5: K4, inc in next 2 sts, K4.

Row 7: K2 tog, K3, inc in next 2 sts, K3, K2 tog.

Row 9: K2 tog, K to last 2 sts, K2 tog (10 sts).

Cont straight in st st until work measures 8cm (3in), ending on a P row.

Mark each end of last row.

TO SHAPE TOP

K2 tog at each end of next and foll alt row (6 sts).

Cast off, purling 2 sts tog at each end of row at same time.

Tail

Starting at tip of tail, cast on 3 sts.

Starting with a K row, inc 1 st at each end of next and foll alt row (7 sts).

St st until work measures 8cm (3in).

Next row: Inc 1 st at each end of row (9 sts).

Continue in st st until tail measures 14cm (5½in).

Cast off.

To make up

Sew in and trim all loose yarn ends. Press all pieces except tail with a warm iron, especially at edges where they tend to curl in. Match all pieces K sides together to sew up unless stated otherwise. Use a small oversew stitch to sew up the pieces.

HEAD

Sew two side pieces together from front neck to tip of nose. Starting from tip of nose (identified by long yarn tail), pin and then sew first one side and then other to head gusset, taking care that both sides are even. Turn RS out. Cut a length of medium brown yarn, pinch end of nose together, wrap middle of yarn around end of nose 3 or 4 times and tie off tightly (this may be a bit fiddly). Trim and thread both ends of yarn onto a tapestry needle and make 3 or 4 satin stitches each way across nose (it does not need to be too neat – these are not posh mice). Sink ends of yarn into head out of sight. Alternatively, tie around nose with body-coloured yarn and carefully colour nose lightly with a brown felt-tip pen. Stuff head carefully, moulding into shape as you go. Leave bottom edges open.

MOUTH

With a length of dark brown embroidery thread, sew an upside down V shape just under the nose for the mouth.

EARS

With RS together, match and sew up ear pieces around outer edges, leaving bottom edges open. Turn RS out and sew closed. Sew to top of head, either side of gusset seam with a pronounced curve. You should then have a gap of about 2cm (¾in) between bottom of each ear.

EYES

You can use either teddy looped-back eyes or small beads. They are both inserted in the same way. Cut a piece of strong black thread about 20cm (7¾in) long and thread one end through an 'eye' or bead, then thread both ends onto a tapestry needle. Push needle down into the position of one eye (about halfway between ears and nose on gusset seam) and bring it out at bottom of head. Do the same with other eye, then pull each pair of threads to embed eyes very slightly into head. Tie the two pairs of threads and knot tightly. Trim ends and tuck them into stuffing out of sight. Use a length of black embroidery thread to sew eyes if giving to a young child.

WHISKERS

Cut a length of extra-strong thread, about 25cm (10in) long. Thread onto the tapestry needle and then double it up. Push needle down into first position, to one side and slightly above nose. Come out directly under nose and pull through until about 2cm (¾in) of threads are left showing. Push needle back in about 1 stitch from where you came out, and bring it out again on other side of nose. Cut threads to match first side. Carefully pull threads apart to separate.

BODY

Fold body lengthways and sew long seam from markers to top; this will be centre back seam. Leave top and bottom open for stuffing later. Turn RS out and set aside.

LEGS

With RS together, fold legs lengthways and sew up seam from back of heel, around feet and up to top of leg. This will be centre front seam. Using forceps or tweezers, turn RS out and stuff to within a centimetre of top. Slip stitch closed. Lay out body with front facing. Sandwich tops of legs just inside bottom of body, with each leg adjacent to sides. Pin and then backstitch the whole bottom edge closed, working through all thicknesses. You should now have a small gap at the back to insert top of tail.

ARMS

With RS together, fold arms lengthways and sew long arm seam from hand up to markers. This will be underarm seam. Turn RS out, stuff carefully and slip stitch the top closed. Sew arms to top of body immediately below shoulder shaping, working from back.

TAIL

Allow tail to curl in naturally lengthways and slip stitch from bottom to top cast off edge. Pinch top edges together and slip stitch closed (the tail is not stuffed). Push cast off end of tail just through gap in body and sew in place, making sure all the bottom seams are now closed. Stuff body firmly but without stretching the knitting out of shape. Position head onto body and sew all around neck, adding a bit more stuffing as you go to keep neck firm.

CLAWS

With tapestry needle and 3 strands of dark brown embroidery thread knotted at the end, take needle and thread into paw, coming out at beginning of first claw position and pulling thread until knotted end disappears into paw. Sew 3 claws and then pull needle out further up the limb. Push needle back into same hole, bring it back out a bit further away, pull thread to create some tension, snip off close to the surface and the thread should disappear into the limb.

Accessories

Scarf

With cream yarn, cast on 5 sts and
K 1 row.
Working in g. st, K 2 rows in red yarn
and 2 rows in cream yarn alternately until
scarf measures 23cm (9in), ending on a
cream row.
Cast off.

FRINGE

Cut 8 lengths of red yarn, 10cm (4in)
long. Fold a piece in half and thread both
ends together onto tapestry needle. Push
needle through an edge stitch at one end
of scarf and then through the loop, which
is formed as you pull the threads through.
Pull tightly to knot. Repeat 3 times evenly
along end of scarf and then do same at
other end. Trim threads to about 1cm
(½in) long.

Skirt

SKIRT TRIM

*With cream yarn, cast on 74 sts.
Break yarn, join in red and g. st 2 rows.**
Starting with a K row, st st 4 rows.
Cast off and set aside.

MAIN SKIRT

Repeat from * to **.
Starting with a K row, st st 4 rows.
K 3 rows.
Next row: P.
Next row: K1, K2 tog to last st, K1
(38 sts).
K 2 rows.
Next row: P.
K 3 rows and cast off.
Press skirt trim well. With RS facing, pin
top edge of trim just under bottom edge
of main skirt. With red yarn, sew through
both layers with a small running stitch just
above cream edging.
Sew up side seam.

BELT

Cut a piece of red yarn about 130cm
(51in) long. Fold in half and, holding both
ends, twist it as tightly as you can and
then fold in half again, keeping cord taut
to avoid tangling. Tie a knot at each end
and trim neatly. Tie around top of skirt
and knot at front.

Necklace

This decoration, or something similar, can
be found in most haberdashery or craft
shops. Simply cut to size and sew at back
to secure. You could also buy small beads
from charity shops or car boot sales and
thread them onto a length of thread.

Lucy

I was asked to knit a version of the Fred and Alice mice (see page 32) in these colours for a friend's daughter. She loved this pretty, 'girly' version.

Mouse and Accessories

Work all parts of mouse as for Fred and Alice using cream yarn plus the following colour changes.

Legs
Cast on and work first 5 rows in dark pink yarn, then change to cream yarn to complete legs. After stuffing, thread tapestry needle with dark pink yarn, double it up and knot the end. Sew over foot from one side of shoe to other. Fasten off. Sew a white bead to outside of each shoe.

Ears
Make 2 of the pieces in light pink yarn for inside of ears. Tie dark pink ribbon between ears after making up.

Skirt
Work in dark pink yarn with light pink edging.
Make main skirt a bit longer by working first 6 rows as for Alice's skirt, then K 3 rows, then complete last 8 rows as for Alice's skirt.

Milly

This cute little dog is very quick and easy to knit. She comes complete with bed, coat, two blankets, a bone and some toys. The thread-jointed legs make her fully poseable and her removable coat can be knitted in the two-colour check pattern or in a single solid colour. This is a great way to use up scraps of yarn left over from other projects.

HEIGHT
Approximately 10cm (4in)

MATERIALS
- 1 x 50g ball DK yarn in medium blue for bed
- Oddments of DK yarn in white and red for dog and coat (use the same brand of yarn to ensure a good fit)
- Oddments of DK yarn in yellow, blue, camel and green for accessories
- Pair of 3mm knitting needles
- Polyester stuffing
- Tapestry/yarn needle
- Two 4mm black beads for eyes
- Black embroidery thread
- 2 tiny press fasteners for coat
- 2 white beads for decorating belt
- Small piece of ribbon for collar (optional)

Dog

Use white yarn throughout.

Body and head
SIDE A
Cast on 8 sts.
Starting with a K row, work in st st.
Row 1: Inc in every st (16 sts).
Row 2: P.
Row 3: K2, (inc 1, K1) to last 2 sts, K2 (22 sts).
Row 4: P.
Row 5: Inc 1 st at each end of row (24 sts).
Row 6: P.
Inc 1 st at end of next and foll 4th row (26 sts).
St st 3 rows, ending on a P row.
Dec 1 st at beg of next and foll alt row (24 sts).
Row 18: P.

TO SHAPE HEAD
Row 19: Cast off 14 sts, K to end (10 sts).
Row 20: Cast on 4 sts, P to end (14 sts).
Row 21: K2 tog, (inc 1, K1) to last 4 sts, K4 (17 sts).

St st 6 rows, ending on a K row.
Row 28: Cast off 6 sts, P to end (11 sts).
Row 29: K.
Row 30: (P2 tog, P1) to last 2 sts, P2 tog (7 sts).
Row 31: K.
Cast off, purling 2 sts tog at each end of row at same time.

SIDE B
Work as for side A to *.
Inc 1 st at beg of next and foll 4th row (26 sts).
St st 4 rows, ending on a K row.
Dec 1 st at beg of next and foll alt row (24 sts).
Row 19: K.

TO SHAPE HEAD
Row 20: Cast off 14 sts at beg of row, P to end (10 sts).
Row 21: Cast on 4 sts at beg of row, K to end.
Row 22: P.
Row 23: K4, (inc 1, K1) to last 2 sts, K2 tog (17 sts).

St st 5 rows, ending on a P row.

Row 29: Cast off 6 sts at beg of row, K to end.

Row 30: P.

Row 31: (K2 tog, K1) to last 2 sts, K2 tog (7 sts).

Row 32: P.

Cast off, knitting 2 sts tog at each end of row at same time.

Ears – make 2

Work in g. st throughout.

Cast on 7 sts and K 2 rows.

Next row: (K1, K2 tog) twice, K1.

Next row: K.

Next row: K2 tog at each end of row (3 sts).

Next row: K1, K2 tog.

K2 tog and fasten off.

Front legs – make 2

Cast on 4 sts.

Starting with a K row, work in st st.

Inc in every st on first and foll alt row (16 sts).

Row 4: P.

Row 5: K6, K2 tog twice, K6.

Row 6: P5, P2 tog twice, P5.

Row 7: K4, K2 tog twice, K4.*

St st 7 rows.

Row 15: (Inc 1, K2, inc 1, K1) twice (14 sts).

St st 3 rows.

Row 19: (K2 tog, K4) twice, K2 tog.

Cast off, purling 2 sts tog at each end of row at same time.

Back legs – make 2

Work as for front legs to *.

St st 5 rows, ending on a P row.

Row 13: Inc 1, K3, inc in next 2 sts, K2, inc 1, K1 (14 sts).

Row 14: P.

Row 15: K6, inc in next 2 sts, K6.

St st 3 rows.

Row 19: K6, K2 tog twice, K6.

Row 20: P2 tog, P3, P2 tog twice, P3, P2 tog (10 sts).

Cast off, knitting 2 sts tog at each end of row at same time.

Tail

Cast on 8 sts and st st 2 rows.

Dec 1 st at each end of next and 2 foll alt rows (2 sts).

P2 tog and fasten off.

To make up

With P sides tog, join sides A and B, oversewing around edges and leaving a gap in tummy. Fold each limb lengthways and sew up, leaving a small gap at back. Turn all pieces RS out and stuff firmly, carefully shaping as you go (you will find a pair of tweezers or forceps very useful for stuffing the limbs). Close gaps with tiny oversew sts. Fold tail and sew along side, turn RS out, add a little stuffing and sew in place.

Neaten ears and sew on as in photograph (facing forwards with a tight curve). Embroider eyes by making tiny sts, one at a time over and over on top of each other, or you could use 4mm beads for eyes if the toy is not for a young child. Pinch and shape paws and sew on claws. Embroider nose and mouth. If you wish to add a collar, cut a length of ribbon, wrap around neck and sew at front.

TO ATTACH LEGS

Pin legs in position on body, then remove them, replacing pins where 'joints' are going to be. Thread a needle with a long piece of white yarn, double it up and knot the end. Sew through body from one front leg 'joint' position to the other, pulling tightly to indent body and fasten off. Do same with back legs.

With another length of yarn, take a few sts from inside tops of legs, go through body to corresponding leg and do the same. Repeat 2 or 3 times, pulling tightly each time. Keep sts close together to allow for maximum movement.

Accessories

Coat

Note: If you think you might find the two-colour check pattern too fiddly, just follow the instructions in one colour; the coat will still look very smart.

With red yarn and starting at tail end, cast on 25 sts.

G. st 3 rows, inc 1 st at each end of first and third rows (29 sts).

Next row: K2 red, join in white, (K1 white, K1 red) to last 2 sts, K2 red.

Next row: K2 red, (P1 red, P1 white) to last 2 sts, K2 red.

Keep check pattern as set and first and last 2 sts in red g. st throughout from now on. Make sure you twist the colours together at beginning of every row to avoid a hole from forming.

Rep last 2 rows 3 times.

Next row: K2, K2 tog, pattern to last 4 sts, K2 tog, K2.

Next row: K2, pattern to last 2 sts, K2.

Rep last 2 rows twice (23 sts).

Work 4 rows straight, ending on a WS row.

Next row: K2, m1, pattern to last 2 sts, m1, K2.

Next row: K2, pattern to last 2 sts, K2.

Rep last 2 rows once (27 sts).

RIGHT SIDE OF NECK

Next row: Pattern 8, K2 tog, turn and work on these sts only for now.

Next row: Pattern to last 2 sts, K2.

Next row: Pattern to last 2 sts, K2 tog.

Rep last 2 rows twice (6 sts).

Work 3 rows straight, ending on a P row.

Break off white.

G. st 3 rows in red and cast off.

LEFT SIDE OF NECK

With RS facing, place next 7 sts on a holder.

Next row: Rejoin red and white yarn, K2 tog, pattern to end.

Next row: K2, pattern to end.

Next row: K2 tog, pattern to end.

Rep last 2 rows twice (6 sts).

Work 3 rows straight, ending on a P row.

Break off white.

G. st 3 rows in red and cast off.

NECK BORDER

With RS facing and red yarn, pick up and K 12 sts along right side of neck (starting at last cast off st), 7 sts on holder and 12 sts along left side of neck (31 sts).

K 1 row and cast off.

Belt

Cast on 3 sts and g. st until belt measures about 15cm (6in) to fit around tummy and overlap by 1cm (½in). Cast off.

Sew half of a press fastener to inside of belt at one end. Sew other half to outside of belt at other end. Sew centre of belt to centre back of coat. Add a couple of beads. Sew press fastener to neck on corresponding sides.

Bed
SIDES

With blue yarn, cast on 110 sts.

Starting with a P row, st st 7 rows.

Cast off 10 sts at beg of next 2 rows (90 sts).

Next row: K1, K2 tog, K to last 3 sts, K2 tog, K1.

Next row: P.

Rep last 2 rows 4 times (80 sts).

Next row: Inc in first and last st.

Next row: P.

Rep last 2 rows 4 times (90 sts).

Cast on 10 sts at beg of next 2 rows (110 sts).

St st 6 rows and cast off.

Press if necessary. With K sides together, fold side of bed end to end and match up the two pairs of opposite, short end pieces (see diagram, below).

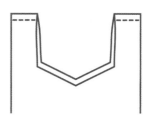

Sew using tiny oversew sts. Keeping K sides together, refold lengthways, match up and sew the shaped front edges, using a small backstitch about 1 st in from edge to hide cast off edges (see diagram, below).

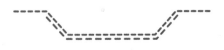

Turn RS out and press seams flat with finger and thumb. Pin and oversew bottom edges together.

BASE

Cast on 14 sts.
Working in g. st throughout, inc in first and last but one st on next and every foll alt row until 28 sts, then every 4th row until 34 sts.
K 6 rows straight.
Dec 1 st at each end of next and every 4th row until 28 sts, then every alt row until 16 sts.
Cast off.
Pin and sew base to side piece, using tiny oversew sts on the outside.

Yellow blanket

Cast on 31 sts.
First row: (K1, P1) to last st, K1.
Continue in moss st by repeating first row until blanket is about square.
Cast off.
Do not press. Blanket st around edges in blue yarn.

Striped blanket

With cream yarn, cast on 30 sts.
Work in st st alternating 2 rows each of cream and camel yarn until blanket is about square. Cast off.
Press if necessary. With P side facing, blanket st around edges in blue yarn.

Bone – make 2 pieces

With camel yarn, cast on 4 sts.
Starting with a K row, work in st st.
First row: Inc 1 st at each end of row (6 sts).
St st 2 rows.
Next row: Dec 1 st at each end of row (4 sts).
St st 12 rows, ending on a P row.
Next row: Inc 1 st at each end of row (6 sts).
St st 2 rows.
Cast off, purling 2 sts tog at each end of row at same time.
With both pieces of bone RS together, sew all around edges, leaving a small gap along one side to turn and stuff. Turn RS out and push some stuffing into ends of bone only. Slip stitch closed.

Plaited toy

Cut 12 lengths from the different-coloured yarns, each about 18cm (7in) long. Bunch them together, then tie and knot them about 2cm (¾in) from one end. Divide longer lengths into 3 bunches and plait for about 4cm (1½in). Tie and knot again, then trim both ends to neaten.

Christmas Reindeer

This pattern is based on the Milly dog instructions (see page 38), with only small changes for the body and limbs. These pretty little reindeer look nice in a group at the end of the mantelpiece, among the festive trimmings.

HEIGHT
Approximately 10cm (4in)

MATERIALS
- 1 x 50g ball 4ply yarn in light brown or fawn
- Pair of 2.75mm knitting needles
- Two 3mm beads for eyes
- Red and black embroidery thread and sewing needle
- Scraps of red and yellow felt
- 4 shirt buttons for each reindeer and matching sewing thread
- 2 pieces of dark brown pipe cleaner or thin jewellery wire wrapped with brown embroidery thread
- Tapestry/yarn needle
- Polyester stuffing
- Gold ribbon, a tiny bell or pretty beads for collar (optional)

Note: I have used 4ply yarn but the reindeer can just as easily be made from DK yarn. Use 3mm knitting needles and make the felt coat a little bit bigger to fit, the antlers a bit longer too, and use 4mm beads for eyes.

Reindeer and Accessories

Body for standing reindeer
SIDE A
Work as for side A of Milly to beginning of head shaping.
Next row: Cast off 14 sts, K to end.
P 1 row.
Cast off.

SIDE B
Work as for side A to beginning of head shaping.
Next row: Cast off 14 sts, P to end.
K 1 row.
Cast off.

Body for sleeping reindeer
SIDE A
Work as for side A of Milly to end of row 6.
Inc 1 st at end of next and foll alt row (26 sts).
Next row: P.
Dec 1 st at end of next and foll 2 alt rows (23 sts).
Next row: P.
Dec 1 st at each end of next and foll alt row (19 sts).

Next row: P.
Cast off.

SIDE B
As for side A, reversing shaping by inc and dec at beg of rows instead of end.

Head for both reindeer
SIDE A
Cast on 10 sts.
P 1 row.
K 1 row.
Cont as for side A of Milly's head from row 20.

SIDE B
Cast on 10 sts.
K 1 row.
P 1 row.
Cont as for side B of Milly's head from row 21.

Front legs
As for Milly but after row 7 work 13 rows straight instead of 7.

Back legs

As for Milly but after row 7 work 11 rows straight instead of 5.

To make up

Sew up and stuff as for Milly but leave neck open. Try not to push any stuffing into toes. Sew up and stuff head and then sew to body with one reindeer looking ahead, one looking around to front and the sleeping reindeer with his head forwards and down. Push a little more stuffing into neck as you go to make it nice and firm. Attach limbs as for Milly, adding shirt buttons if required. Insert eyes as for Milly and embroider nose and mouth using 3 strands of black embroidery thread (red for Rudolph).

EARS

Knit as for Milly. Neaten and trim off cast on thread. Weave cast off thread down side of ear. Fold ear in half lengthways and sew to head as in photograph. A pin pushed down middle of ear into head will hold the ear in place while you sew it.

TAIL

As for Milly.

ANTLERS

Cut two pieces of pipe cleaner, one 12cm (4¾in) long and one 8cm (3in) long. Bend longest one into a horseshoe shape with a flattened bottom edge. Do the same with the shorter piece and then twist the two ends around the longer piece using diagram, right, and photograph as a guide. With reindeer-coloured yarn, oversew to top of head between ears.

COAT

Cut a 6 x 3cm (2½ x 1in) piece of red felt and a 7 x 3.5cm (2¾ x 1¼in) piece of yellow felt for each reindeer. Place yellow piece and then red piece on reindeer's back. Cut a strip of yellow felt about 14cm (5½in) long. Wrap around tummy, overlap a little bit and secure with a bead or button. Sew some gold ribbon around neck and a tiny bell or pretty beads to front.

Shape and twist the two pieces of pipe cleaner together for the antlers.

Glove Puppets and Their Babies

The two pairs of glove puppet adults (see also photograph on page 56) are fairly easy to make but the babies' heads are a bit fiddly, and are not suitable for very young children because of the small parts.

HEIGHT
Puppets: approximately 25cm (10in)
Babies: approximately 14cm (5½in)

MATERIALS FOR
MATILDA BEAR, MAISY DOG AND BABIES
- 1 x 50g ball DK yarn in gold for Matilda Bear and baby plus oddment of blue for baby
- 1 x 25g ball DK yarn in each of cream and light brown for Maisy Dog and puppy

MATERIALS FOR
BEATRICE BADGER, FREYA FOX AND BABIES
- 1 x 50g ball DK yarn in black for Bertha Badger and baby, plus oddment of dark grey for baby
- 1 x 50g ball DK yarn in tan for Freya Fox and cub

PLUS, FOR ALL TOYS
- 1 x 50g ball DK yarn in cream for all four sets of toys
- Oddments of DK yarn for blankets and sleeping bags
- Pair of 3mm knitting needles for adults
- Pair of 2.75mm knitting needles for babies plus spare needle of same size or smaller for working muzzle
- Pair of 4mm knitting needles for accessories
- Polyester stuffing
- Tapestry/yarn needle
- Oddment of brown felt for paw pads and matching sewing thread
- Two 9–10mm black safety eyes for badger, 10mm teddy safety eyes for other adults and 3mm black beads for babies
- Black and brown embroidery thread
- Forceps or tweezers for stuffing babies
- 3 buttons and 2 press fasteners for each sleeping bag
- Embellishments such as lace and ribbons

Matilda Bear

Body – make 2 pieces
With gold, cast on 32 sts and K 3 rows.
Starting with a P row, st st 33 rows.
Inc 1 st at each end of next and every foll alt row until 48 sts.
Next row: P.

TO SHAPE FIRST PAW
Next row: K13, turn and work on these sts only for now, P2 tog, P to end.
Next row: K.
Dec 1 st at beg of next and foll alt row (10 sts).
Dec 1 st at each end of next and foll alt row (6 sts).
Cast off purlwise.

TO SHAPE NECK
With RS facing, rejoin yarn, K2 tog, K18, K2 tog, turn and work on these 20 sts only for now.
P 1 row.

Next row: K2 tog, K to last 2 sts, K2 tog
(18 sts).
P I row and cast off.

TO SHAPE SECOND PAW

With RS facing, rejoin yarn and K to end.
Dec I st at end of next and 2 foll alt rows
(10 sts).
Dec I st at each end of next and foll alt
row (6 sts).
Cast off purlwise.

Head

With gold and starting at back of head,
cast on 18 sts and P I row.
Starting with a K row, work in st st, inc
I st at each end of next and foll alt row
(22 sts).
St st 15 rows straight, ending on a P row.

TO SHAPE TOP OF HEAD

Dec I st at each end of next 6 rows
(10 sts).
Inc I st at each end of next 6 rows
(22 sts).
St st 6 rows straight.

TO SHAPE MUZZLE

Next row: K17, turn, P12, mark next st,
turn and work on centre 12 sts only for
now.
Starting with a K row, st st 2 rows.
Dec I st at each end of next and every
foll alt row until 6 sts, ending on a P row.
Break off yarn.
With RS facing, rejoin yarn at marker, pick
up and K 8 sts along first side of muzzle,
K across 6 sts of nose on needle, pick up
and K 8 sts along second side of muzzle,

K to end (32 sts).
Starting with a P row, st st 7 rows.
Next row: K2 tog, K12, K2 tog twice,
K12, K2 tog (28 sts).
Next row: P.
Next row: K2 tog, K10, K2 tog twice,
K10, K2 tog (24 sts).
Next row: P.
Cont to dec in this way until 20 sts.
Next row: K8, K2 tog twice, K8 (18 sts).
Cast off purlwise.

HEAD BASE

With gold, cast on 4 sts.
Starting with a K row, work in st st, inc
I st at each end of every row until 10 sts.
St st 11 rows straight.
Dec I st at each end of every row until
4 sts.
Cast off.

Ears – make 4 pieces

With gold, cast on 9 sts and P I row.
Next row: Inc I st at each end of row
(11 sts).
St st 2 rows.
Dec I st at each end of next 3 rows
(5 sts).
Cast off, knitting 2 sts tog at each end of
row at same time and leave long yarn tail.
With WS together, sew 2 ear pieces
together around shaped edge, leaving
bottom edge open. Turn RS out and
oversew bottom edge. Repeat for
second ear.

To make up
HEAD

With RS together, fold and sew up
sides of head. Turn RS out. Stuff head
temporarily and position eyes (try
different positions or refer to photograph).
When you are happy with them, carefully
remove them and mark where eye shanks
are to go.
Remove enough stuffing to fit eyes and
safety backing, then finish stuffing head
firmly, filling the muzzle and moulding the
head as you go. Stitch a nose and mouth.
Pin and sew front of head base to front of
head, leaving back edge open so that little
fingers can fit in to nod the puppet's head.
Position ears using pins and then sew
to head.

BODY

With RS together, sew body pieces
together. Turn RS out. Using template
below, cut out paw pads and sew to
paws, taking care not to go through both
layers. Sew head to body around neck,
being careful not to catch the open back
edge of head base in your sts. Add a
pretty piece of cotton lace and a small
flower for a shawl.

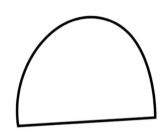

Matilda's paw pads.

Body

With dark grey, cast on 22 sts.
Next row: K5, turn and P back.
K3, turn and P back.
Next row: K10, inc in next 2 sts, K10 (24 sts).
Next row: P5, turn and K back.
P3, turn and K back.*
St st 19 rows straight.

TO SHAPE SHOULDERS

Next row: K5, K2 tog twice, K6, K2 tog twice, K5 (20 sts).
Next row: P.
Next row: K5, K2 tog, K6, K2 tog, K5 (18 sts).
Cast off purlwise.

Front legs – make 2

With black and starting at paws, cast on 4 sts.
First row: Inc in every st (8 sts).
Next row: P.
Next row: K2, K2 tog twice, K2 (6 sts).
St st 5 rows.*
Next row: Inc 1 st at each end of row (8 sts).
St st 5 rows.
Break off yarn, draw through sts, pull up tightly and fasten off.

Back legs – make 2

Work as for front legs to *.
Inc 1 st at each end of next and 2 foll alt rows (12 sts).
P 1 row.
Fasten off as for front legs.

Tail

With cream, cast on 8 sts and P 1 row.
Dec 1 st at each end of next and foll alt row.
Break off yarn, draw through sts, pull up tightly and fasten off.

To make up
BODY AND HEAD

With K side tog, fold and sew up long (back) seam of body. Refold so that back seam is central and sew up bottom cast on edges. Sew up side seams of head, leaving neck open. Turn RS out and stuff firmly, carefully shaping nose, bottom and shoulders. Sew head to body. Attach beads for eyes or embroider. Stitch a nose and mouth with black thread.

EARS

Knot and anchor a length of black yarn just down from one corner of head, then take another st diagonally up to top of head. Pinch corner together firmly, wrap yarn around tightly and fasten off with another couple of sts. Repeat on other side. With a length of cream yarn, sew a couple of large sts across top of each ear.

LEGS

With WS together, fold and sew up limbs, stuffing top and middle of legs just before closing seam. With a finger and thumb, flatten paws firmly so that seam runs up centre back of legs.
In seated position, pin back legs to body, then carefully remove and mark with pins where legs will go. Sew to body by taking a stitch from inside top of one leg, go through body to other 'joint' position and take a stitch from second leg. Repeat a couple of times to secure.

TAIL

With P side together, fold in half lengthways and oversew side seam on RS. The tail is not stuffed. Taking care not to flatten tail, position and sew on by stitching around cast off edges.

Freya Fox

Body

Work as for Matilda Bear using cream for front of body and tan for back.

Head

With tan only and ignoring colour changes, work as for adult badger to *.
St st 8 rows straight, ending on a P row.

TO SHAPE MUZZLE

Next row: K14, turn, P6, mark next st, turn and work on centre 6 sts only for now.
Starting with a K row, st st 12 rows.
Next row: K2 tog, K to last 2 sts, K2 tog (4 sts).
P 1 row and break off yarn.
With RS facing, rejoin yarn at marker, pick up and K 11 sts along first side of muzzle, K across 4 sts of nose on needle, pick up and K 11 sts along second side of muzzle, K to end (42 sts).
Break off tan and join in cream.
Starting with a P row, st st 2 rows.

Next row: P24, turn.
Sl 1, K4, K2 tog, turn.
Sl 1, P4, P2 tog, turn.
Sl 1, K5, K2 tog, turn.
Sl 1, P6, P2 tog, turn.
Sl 1, K7, K2 tog, turn.
Sl 1, P8, P2 tog, turn.
Cont to dec in this way until 28 sts, ending on a P row. P to end.
Next row: K2 tog, K10, K2 tog twice, K10, K2 tog (24 sts).
Next row: P.
Next row: K2 tog, K8, K2 tog twice, K8, K2 tog (20 sts).
Next row: P.
Next row: Dec 1 st at each end of row (18 sts).
P 1 row and cast off.

HEAD BASE

Work as for Matilda Bear using tan.

Ears
INNER EARS – MAKE 2

With cream, cast on 12 sts.
Starting with a K row, st st 4 rows.*
Next row: K1, K2 tog, K to last 3 sts, K2 tog, K1 (10 sts).
Next row: P.
Rep last 2 rows until 4 sts.
Next row: K2 tog twice.
Next row: P2 tog and fasten off.

OUTER EARS – MAKE 2

With tan, cast on 12 sts.
Starting with a K row, st st 2 rows.
Next row: Join in black and K1 black, K1 tan alternately across row.
Break off tan and cont in black only.
P 1 row.
Complete as for inner ears from *.

TO JOIN INNER AND OUTER EARS

With K sides together and using tiny sts, sew around sides of ears. Turn RS out and sew up bottom edges.

Tail

With tan yarn, cast on 10 sts.
Inc 1 st at each end of every row until 20 sts.
St st straight until tail measures 11cm (4¼in), ending on a P row.
Dec 1 st at each end of next and every foll 4th row until 12 sts.
Next row: Join in cream and K1 cream, K1 tan alternately across row.
Break off tan and cont in cream, dec as before until 4 sts remain.
Break off yarn, thread through remaining sts and fasten off.

Fold and sew up seam, then refold so seam is at centre underside of tail.

To make up

Make up head and body as for Matilda Bear but use same paw pads template as Maisy Dog. Sew tail to body (I attached it with a large brown button). Dress her in a collar and string of beads.

Fox Cub

Head

With tan and starting at back of head, cast on 8 sts.
First row: Inc 1 st at each end of row (10 sts).
Starting with a P row, st st 7 rows straight.
Dec 1 st at end of next 2 rows (8 sts).
Inc 1 st at end of next 2 rows (10 sts).
St st 4 rows straight.

TO SHAPE MUZZLE

Next row: K7, turn, P4, mark next st, turn and work on centre 4 sts only for now.
St st 4 rows.
Next row: K2 tog twice (2 sts).
Next row: P.
Break off yarn.
With RS facing, join in cream at marker, pick up and K 5 sts along first side of muzzle, K across 2 sts of nose on needle, with spare needle pick up and K 5 sts along second side of muzzle, K to end (18 sts).
Revert to original needles.
Next row: P.

Next row: K10, turn.
P2, turn.
Sl 1, K2 tog, turn.
Sl 1, P2 tog, turn.
Rep last 2 rows twice (12 sts).
K to end.
P 1 row.
Next row: K2 tog, K2, K2 tog twice, K2, K2 tog (8 sts).
P 1 row and cast off.

Body

Wind off a small ball of tan yarn for later. With main ball of tan, work as for Baby Badger to *.
St st 9 rows straight.
Next row: K11, join in cream and K2, K11 tan (use spare ball and twist yarns together at every colour change).
Next row: P11 tan, P2 cream, P11 tan.
Next row: K10 tan, K4 cream, K10 tan.
Next row: P10 tan, P4 cream, P10 tan.*
Cont widening the cream patch in this way until there are 10 cream sts, ending on a P row.
Keeping colours as set, complete as for Baby Badger from start of shoulder shaping.

Front legs – make 2

With black, cast on 4 sts and work as for Baby Badger to *.
Change to tan.
Next row: Inc 1 st at each end of row (8 sts).
St st 9 rows straight.
Break off yarn, draw through sts, pull up tightly and fasten off.

Back legs – make 2

Work as for front legs to *.
St st 2 rows.
Change to tan.
Inc 1 st at each end of next and 2 foll alt rows (12 sts).
St st 4 rows straight.
Fasten off as for front legs.

Ears – make 2

With tan, cast on 6 sts and K 1 row.
Next row: P.
Next row: K2 tog, K2, K2 tog (4 sts).
Next row: P.
Next row: K2 tog twice (2 sts).
Next row: P2 tog and fasten off, leaving a long tail.

Tail

With tan, cast on 4 sts and st st 2 rows.
Inc 1 st at each end of every row until 12 sts.
St st 8 rows straight.
Dec 1 st at each end of next and every foll 4th row until 8 sts.
St st 3 rows.
Change to cream and cont to dec until 4 sts.
P 1 row.
Next row: K2 tog twice (2 sts).
Break off yarn, thread through sts, pull up tightly and fasten off.

To make up
BODY AND HEAD

Make up body, head and face as for Baby Badger. With cream, darn 3 or 4 sts across front central part of ears and then sew ears to head.

Legs

Sew up limbs on RS, stuffing as you go. Attach to body in same way as for Baby Badger.

Tail

Fold and sew up seam on RS to within 2 rows of top. In seated position, pin tail into place with seam underneath, then sew on.

Accessories
Blankets

With 4mm needles, cast on 22 sts and work in g. st until blanket is square. Blanket stitch the edges in a contrast colour.

Sleeping bags

With 4mm needles, cast on 36 sts and work in g. st for about 8cm (3in).
Next row: Cast off 16 sts, K to end.
Next row: K.
K2 tog at each end of next and every foll 4th row until 10 sts.
K 1 row and cast off.
Fold and sew up bottom cast on edge to form the open bag. Turn RS out and use contrast colour to blanket stitch all around the open edges. Sew daisy stitch (see page 91) on centre front of bag and sew a pretty button to centre of daisy. Sew press fasteners to side edges for closing (and tiny buttons on top if required).

Miniature Dolls

These are ideal as little dressing up dolls. Their clothes are very easy to get on and off. They have shaped bottoms so are able to sit comfortably. Their small size makes them perfect for using up leftover yarn from other projects.

HEIGHT
Approximately 16cm (6¼in)

MATERIALS
- Oddments of DK yarn in flesh colour for dolls, plus various colours for hair, shoes and socks
- Oddments of 4ply yarn in various colours for rest of clothes
- Brown or black and red or pink embroidery thread
- Pair each of 3mm, 2.75mm and 2.25mm knitting needles
- Tapestry/yarn needle
- Polyester stuffing
- 2 beads for dress
- 4 beads or tiny buttons and press fasteners for cardigan (optional)
- Press fastener for jumper and skirt
- Ribbon or other hair embellishments
- Forceps or tweezers for turning and stuffing limbs

Dolls

Work in st st unless stated otherwise.

Body and head
With 3mm needles and flesh colour, cast on 24 sts.
First row: K6, (inc 1, K3) 3 times, K6 (27 sts).
Next row: P.

TO SHAPE BOTTOM
K2, turn and P back.
K4, turn, sl 1, P back.
K6, turn, sl 1, P back.
K8, turn, sl 1, P back.
Next row: K to end.
P2, turn and K back.
P4, turn, sl 1, K back.
P6, turn, sl 1, K back.
P8, turn, sl 1, K back.
Next row: P to end.
Dec 1 st at each end of next and foll alt row (23 sts).
*St st 9 rows, ending on a P row.

TO SHAPE SHOULDERS AND HEAD
Next row: K4, K2 tog twice, K7, K2 tog twice, K4.
Next row: P.

Next row: K4, K2 tog, K7, K2 tog, K4 (17 sts).**
St st 3 rows.
Next row: K4, inc in next 8 sts, K5 (25 sts).
St st 10 rows, ending on a K row.
Next row: P2 tog to last st, P1.
Next row: K2 tog to last st, K1 (7 sts).
Break yarn, leaving a long enough thread to sew up back seam of head and body, thread through remaining sts and draw up tightly.

Legs – make 2
These instructions are for legs wearing shoes and socks. See overleaf for legs wearing shoes and striped tights.
With 3mm needles and shoe colour, cast on 18 sts.
Starting with a P row, st st 3 rows.
Row 4: K3, K3 tog 4 times, K3 (10 sts).
Change to sock colour.
Row 5: P tightly.*
Row 6: K3, K2 tog twice, K3.
St st 2 rows, ending on a K row.
Row 9: K.
Change to flesh colour.
Starting with a K row, st st 6 rows.

Next row: Inc 1, K7 (9 sts).
St st 7 rows straight.
Cast off.

STRIPED TIGHTS

To work legs wearing pink-and-white striped tights, start with shoe colour and work legs as above to end of row 4.
Change to white and P tightly.
Work row 6.
Change to pink and st st 2 rows, ending on a K row.
Change to white and P row 9 instead of knitting it.
Cont in 2-row stripes for 6 rows, then work the inc row and remaining 7 rows.

Arms – make 2

Starting with hands, with 3mm needles and flesh colour, cast on 6 sts.
Start with a K row.
First row: K1, inc in next 4 sts, K1 (10 sts).
Next row: P.
Next row: K3, K2 tog twice, K3.
Next row: P3, P2 tog, P3 (7 sts).*
St st 10 rows, ending on a P row.

TO SHAPE TOP

K2 tog at each end of next and foll alt row.
Cast off, slipping first st and leaving enough thread to sew to body.

To make up
HEAD AND BODY

With RS together, sew up centre back seam from cast on edge to top of head, leaving a gap at back for stuffing. Leave bottom edge open. Turn RS out and stuff head and shoulders quite firmly. Tie a length of flesh-coloured yarn around neck, just under increase row, pull up tightly and fasten off. With a tapestry needle, tease out chin and cheek areas to make them nice and chubby. Leave rest of body unstuffed.

LEGS

With RS together, fold legs lengthways and with matching yarn sew up back seam from under foot to about three-quarters up leg. Turn RS out. Stuff shoes with some shoe colour yarn, cut into 2 or 3cm (1in) pieces.
Tease shoes into a nice shape with tapestry needle. Finish sewing back leg seam (on RS) to top and then stuff legs to within 1cm (½in) of top. With seam at centre back, sandwich and pin top of legs between lower edges of body, adjacent to sides and with a small gap in between. Backstitch through all layers. Finish stuffing body and close gap in back seam.

ARMS

With RS together, fold each arm lengthways and sew up underarm seams to start of arm shaping. Turn RS out and stuff lightly to within 1cm (½in) of top. Oversew shaped edges closed at top of arms and then sew to sides of body just below shoulders.

CURLY HAIR

With 3mm needles and chosen hair colour, cast on 24 sts and K 1 row.
First row (WS): K1, *insert right needle

Oversew arms to body with tiny sts, working from the back.

knitwise into next st, place left forefinger behind left needle and wind yarn anticlockwise around the needle and your finger twice (to form curl), draw through the 2 loops (keeping curl on finger at back of work) but, before slipping st off left needle, twist right needle over and K into back of it. Release curl. Rep from * to last st, K1.
Next row (RS): K1, K3 tog to last st, K1 (24 sts).
Rep last 2 rows twice.
Note: Forming the curls is a bit tricky to

Work the curls on WS rows. Keeping curl on finger, draw the two loops through the next stitch.

start with but becomes much easier after the first couple of rows. Try to keep your work fairly loose.

Next row: K2 tog across row.

Break yarn a good length from the work, thread through remaining sts, pull up tightly and fasten off securely. Fold hair RS together and sew up row ends from back to front cast on edge to form a little cap. Turn RS out and fit onto doll, carefully stretching into place around back of head. With another length of yarn, sew around edges and a few sts here and there through the scalp. You can either leave the hair as it is for nice big curls or trim it close to head for a short boy hairstyle.

STRAIGHT HAIR

Cut about 35 lengths of yarn, about 22cm (8½in) long. Working with 4 or 5 pieces at a time, backstitch centre of yarn lengths to seam line at back of head, starting 1cm (½in) up from neck and finishing just above forehead.

To make a fringe, bring forwards some of the hair and trim to about 1cm (½in). Sew some more strands over top of fringe to stop it from sticking up. Gather each side of hair, tie into bunches and secure to head with 2 or 3 sts midway between top and bottom of head. Trim neatly and tie on ribbon. For plaits, use three sets of 4 strands; any more will be too bulky.

EYES

Use pins (black-headed if you have them) to mark where eyes are going to be. Cut a length of embroidery thread, brown

for the light skin tone and black for the darker shade. Use 2 strands. Take thread through back of neck and out at first first eye position. Make 1 tiny st, about half the size of a knit st, and then oversew this st several times. Do not try to spread out; the eyes will build up to the required size (with eyes, less is better than more). Take thread through to second eye position and repeat. If you want eyelashes, make 2 tiny sts with 1 strand of thread.

The mouth is just 2 sts using 1 strand of red or pink embroidery or sewing thread. The nose is 2 tiny sts with 1 strand of light brown (or a couple of dots with a brown felt-tip pen if you have one).

Accessories

Dress

With 3mm needles and 4ply yarn, cast on 60 sts.

G. st 2 rows.

Next row: Join in contrast colour and K 1 st each alternately in the two colours.

Next row: P, alternating colours again. Break off contrast colour.

Starting with a K row, st st 12 rows.

Next row: K2 tog to end (30 sts).*

Next row: K.

Starting with a K row, st st 4 rows.

FRONT

Next row: K2 tog, K11, K2 tog, turn and work on these sts only for now.

Next row: K2, P to last 2 sts, K2.

Next row: K2, K2 tog, K to last 4 sts, K2 tog, K2.

Keeping first and last 2 sts K in every row, st st 4 rows straight, ending on a K row.**

G. st 2 rows.
Cast off.

BACK

With RS facing, rejoin yarn to remaining sts.

Next row: K2 tog, K to last 2 sts, K2 tog.

Next row: K2, P to last 2 sts, K2.

Next row: K2, K2 tog, K to last 4 sts, K2 tog, K2.

Keeping first and last 2 sts K in every row, st st 6 rows, ending on a K row.

G. st 2 rows.

Next row: K3, cast off next 5 sts, K to end.

SHOULDER STRAPS

You should now have two sets of 3 sts on the needle for the shoulder straps.

G. st 12 rows on first set of sts. Cast off. Rejoin yarn and repeat for second strap. Sew up side seam of dress to **.

Fit dress onto doll, bring shoulder straps forwards and sew to front of dress as in photograph. Sew 2 beads in place.

Note: If you want to be able to remove the dress, sew press fasteners to straps and dress.

Cardigan
BACK AND FRONT TO ARMHOLES

With 2.25mm needles and 4ply yarn, cast on 45 sts and work in rib for 2 rows. Change to 2.75mm needles.

Next row: K.

Next row: K2, P to last 2 sts, K2.

Repeat last 2 rows twice.

RIGHT FRONT

K10, K2 tog, turn and work on these sts only for now.

Row 1: P to last 2 sts, K2.

Row 2: K to last 2 sts, K2 tog.

Rep last 2 rows until 8 sts remain.

Next row: P to last 2 sts, K2.

Next row: K2, K2 tog, K2, K2 tog.

Next row: P to last 2 sts, turn.

Next row: K2 tog twice.

Next row: P2 tog and fasten off.

Leave remaining 2 border sts on a safety pin. Break yarn.

BACK

With RS facing, rejoin yarn.

Next row: K2 tog, K17, K2 tog, turn.

Next row: P.

Dec 1 st at each end of next and foll alt rows until 9 sts.

Next row: P to end of row.

Break yarn and leave sts on a holder.

LEFT FRONT

With RS facing, rejoin yarn to remaining sts.

Next row: K2 tog, K to end.

Next row: K2, P to end.

Repeat last 2 rows until 8 sts remain, ending on a P row.

Next row: K2 tog, K2, K2 tog, K2.

Next row: K2, place these sts on a safety pin, P to end.

Next row: K2 tog twice.

Next row: P2 tog and fasten off.

SLEEVES – MAKE 2

With 2.25mm needles, cast on 16 sts and work 2 rows in rib.

Change to 2.75mm needles.

Starting with a K row, st st 2 rows.

Next row: Inc 1, K to last 2 sts, inc 1, K1 (18 sts).

St st 5 rows.

Mark each end of last row.*

K2 tog at each end of next and every foll alt row until 6 sts.

Next row: P to end of row.

Break yarn and leave sts on a holder.

TO MAKE UP

Sew up underarm seams of sleeves to markers. With RS together, match up and sew raglan seams.

With RS facing and 2.25mm needles, K the 2 sts on holder at right front, pick up and K 4 sts along right front then K across right sleeve, then K across back and then left sleeve, pick up and K 4 sts along left front, K 2 sts from holder (33 sts).**

Rib 1 row.

Cast off in rib.

Sew on beads or tiny buttons and corresponding press fasteners if you want the cardigan to fasten.

Jacket

Using 2.75mm needles for the rib and 3mm needles for the main parts, work as for cardigan to **.

Change to 2.75mm needles.

Next row: (Rib 7, K2 tog) 3 times, rib 6 (30 sts).
Next row: Rib to end.

HOOD

Change to 3mm needles.
Starting with a K row and keeping first and last 2 sts K on every row, st st 15 rows.
Next row: K13, K2 tog twice, K13.
Next row: K2, P to last 2 sts, K2.
Next row: K12, K2 tog twice, K12.
Cont to dec 2 sts in middle of every K row until 20 sts remain, ending on a P row.
To cast off, K10, fold back hood with RS together and needles parallel with each other. Cast off 1 st from each needle at same time using a spare needle.

Jumper
FRONT

With 2.25mm needles and 4ply yarn, cast on 20 sts and work in rib for 2 rows.
Change to 2.75mm needles.
Starting with a K row, st st 6 rows.*
Mark each end of last row.

TO SHAPE RAGLAN SLEEVES

K2 tog at each end of next and every foll alt row until 10 sts remain, ending on a P row.
Next row: K2 tog, K1, K2 tog, turn and P back.
Break yarn and leave these 3 sts on a holder.
With RS facing, rejoin yarn to remaining sts, K2 tog, K1, K2 tog.
Next row: P.
Leave remaining sts on a holder.

BACK

Work as for front to *.
Next row: K2 tog, K8, turn and work on these sts only for now.
Next row: K2, P to end.
Next row: K2 tog, K to end.
Next row: K2, P to end.
Repeat last 2 rows 4 times (4 sts).
Break yarn and leave sts on a holder.
With RS facing, rejoin yarn.
Next row: Cast on 2 sts at beg of row, K to last 2 sts, K2 tog.
Mark end of last row.
Next row: P to last 2 sts, K2.
Next row: K to last 2 sts, K2 tog.
Next row: P to last 2 sts, K2.
Rep last 2 rows 4 times (6 sts).
Leave sts on a holder.

SLEEVES – MAKE 2

Make as for cardigan sleeves, leaving sts on a holder.
Join sleeve underarm seams up to markers. Sew up all raglan seams.

NECK

With RS facing and 2.25mm needles, starting at left back, K across 6 sts of left back, 6 sts of left sleeve, 3 sts of left front, pick up and K 4 sts around front neck, K across 3 sts of right front, 6 sts of right sleeve and then 4 sts of right back (32 sts).
Work 2 rows in single rib.
Cast off in rib.
Neaten bottom of back opening with 2 or 3 sts. Sew a press fastener to opening.
Note: You may have to put jumper onto doll feet first, especially the doll with curly hair.

Shorts
RIGHT SIDE

With 2.25mm needles, cast on 18 sts and rib 2 rows.
Change to 2.75mm needles.*
Next row: K3, turn and P back.
Next row: K6, turn and P back.
Next row: K9, turn and P back.
Next row: K across all sts.
Continue in st st for 9 rows, ending on a P row.
Mark each end of last row.
Next row: Inc 1 st at each end of next and foll alt row (22 sts).
Next row: P.**
G. st 3 rows.
Cast off.

LEFT SIDE

Work as for right side to *.
Next row: P3, turn and K back.
Next row: P6, turn and K back.
Next row: P9, turn and K back.
Next row: P across all sts.
St st 8 rows. Mark each end of last row and then complete as for right side.

Trousers

Work as for shorts up to **.
St st 13 more rows, ending on a K row.
K 1 row and cast off.
With RS together, fold each leg in half lengthways and sew up inside leg seam (widest part is the legs). Turn one leg RS out and fit this inside other leg. Sew up crotch seam and turn RS out.

Skirt

Work as for skirt of dress from beginning to *, ignoring the 2 contrast rows and just working the 12 rows of st st (30 sts).
G. st 3 rows and cast off.
With RS together, join skirt seam about three-quarters of the way up to waistband. Sew a press fastener to waistband to close.

Knickers

With 2.25mm needles and 4ply yarn, cast on 18 sts and rib 2 rows.
Change to 2.75mm needles.
Starting with a K row, st st 6 rows.
Next row: K1, K2 tog, K to last 3 sts, K2 tog, K1.
Next row: K1, P2 tog, P to last 3 sts, P2 tog, K1.
Cont to dec in this way until 4 sts remain.
St st 3 rows.
Next row: Inc 1, K to last 2 sts, inc 1, K1.
Next row: Inc 1 knitwise, P to last 2 sts, inc 1, K1.

Cont to inc in this way until 18 sts.
Next row: P.

TO SHAPE BOTTOM

K to last 2 sts, turn.
Sl 1, P to last 2 sts, turn.
Sl 1, K to last 4 sts, turn.
Sl 1, P to last 4 sts, turn.
Sl 1, K to end.
St st 5 rows, ending on a P row.
Change to 2.25mm needles.
Work in single rib for 2 rows.
Cast off in rib.
With RS together, fold and sew up side seams.
Note: The knickers and trousers are not really meant to be worn at the same time as they might be a bit too bulky.

Baseball cap

With 3mm needles, cast on 35 sts and K 1 row.
Starting with a K row, st st 10 rows.
Next row: (K2 tog, K3) to end.

Next row: (P2, P2 tog) to end.
Next row: (K2 tog, K1) to end.
Next row: P2 tog to end (7 sts).
Next row: K2 tog to last st, K1.
Cut yarn, thread through remaining sts, pull up and fasten off.
Sew up seam to form main part of cap.

PEAKED BRIM

With 2.25mm needles, hold cap upside down and pick up 16 sts around front of cap.
Starting with a K row, dec 1 st at each end of next and every foll alt row until 8 sts.
Next row: P.
Next row: Inc 1, K to last 2 sts, inc 1, K1.
Next row: P.
Cont to inc on next and every foll alt row until 18 sts.
K 1 row and cast off.
With RS together, fold brim and oversew each side, turn RS out and oversew to main cap. Press brim firmly between finger and thumb and make tiny stab sts

very close to edge and then along where peak joins cap. This stitching will flatten and give extra stiffening to the peak.

Backpack

With 3mm needles and 4ply yarn, cast on 14 sts.
Starting with a K row, work in st st until knitting measures 9cm (3½in), ending on a P row. Mark each end of last row.

FLAP

Row 1: K.
Row 2: K2, P to last 2 sts, P2.
Row 3: K2, K2 tog, K to last 4 sts, K2 tog, K2.
Row 4: Rep row 2.
Rep last 4 rows twice (8 sts).
G. st 2 rows.
Cast off, knitting 2 sts tog at each end of row at same time.
With RS together, fold rectangle with cast on edges meeting markers and sew sides. Turn RS out.

CORD

Cut a piece of yarn about 40cm (15¾in) long and thread onto a tapestry needle. Holding each end of thread, with needle at centre, twist up tightly and then double up. Knot the end. Sew cord as a small running stitch all around top edge of backpack under markers, starting and finishing at centre front and leaving a couple of centimetres length at each end for ties. Knot and trim end of cord.

STRAPS – MAKE 2

With 2.25mm needles, cast on 3 sts and g. st until strap measures 11cm (4¼in). Cast off.
Sew both ends of each strap to centre top of back of bag.

Sew straps to backpack.

Pixies, Elves and a Leprechaun

The bodies for these little characters are based on the Miniature Dolls (see page 58), but their clothes are knitted in DK yarn rather than 4ply. The pixies and elves are made up in the same way as each other but their boots and hats are different. Pixies also tend to wear a pretty collar (see page 70), while elves generally wear waistcoats and jackets.

HEIGHT
Approximately 20cm (7¾in)

MATERIALS FOR ALL
- Oddments of DK yarn in flesh pink, green, gold, yellow, red, black, tan, white, brown and light cream
- Pair of 3mm knitting needles
- Polyester stuffing
- Dark brown and red embroidery thread and sewing needle
- Tapestry/yarn needle
- 3mm silver or gold beads for buttons for jacket
- Tiny beads for boots and necklace
- Tiny bell for hat
- 2 small buttons for waistcoat
- Forceps or tweezers for turning and stuffing

PLUS, FOR LEPRECHAUN
- 1 x 25g ball DK yarn in green
- Black embroidery thread

Pixies and Elves

The colours stated are for the green, yellow and red pixie. Refer to photographs for other colour combinations. Unless stated otherwise, work in st st throughout, starting with a K row.

Body and head
With green yarn, work as for Miniature Dolls, but work 11 rows st st at * instead of 9 and change to flesh-coloured yarn at **. Sew up as for dolls.

Arms – make 2
Work as for Miniature Dolls to *.
Change to yellow yarn and K 2 rows.
Starting with a K row, st st 8 rows.
Complete as for dolls from beginning of top of arm shaping.
Sew up as for dolls.

Pixie legs – make 2
TO SHAPE BOOTS
With yellow yarn, cast on 20 sts.
First row: K7, K2 tog 3 times, K7 (17 sts).
Next row: P6, P2 tog 3 times, P5.
Next row: K5, K2 tog twice, K5 (12 sts).
Next row: P4, P2 tog twice, P4 (10 sts).
Next row: K4, K2 tog, K4 (9 sts).
St st 2 rows, ending on a K row.
Next row: K.

TO SHAPE LEGS
To work plain tights, change to red yarn.
Starting with a K row, st st 10 rows.
Next row: K4, m1, K5 (10 sts).
St st 9 rows.
Cast off.
Sew up as for Miniature Dolls but stuff only very lightly to within 2cm (¾in) of top. Sew two beads to instep.

Next row: K1, K2 tog.
Next row: P2 tog and fasten off as for left ear.

TO ATTACH EARS TO HEAD

Neaten and snip off cast on thread at top of both ears. With cast off thread (at bottom of ear) and K side facing, sew straight side edge of ears (see diagram, below) to either side of head working from back of ear.

Hair for both

With light brown yarn, sew some tacking sts from centre top of head down to forehead (see below diagram). With tip of a pin, rough up and split the sts a little bit.

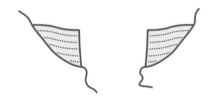

Right and left ears showing cast on threads at top and cast off threads at bottom.

For the longer, striped legs of the other pixie (see page 70), work the tights in 2-row stripes and add an extra 4 rows.

Elf legs – make 2
TO SHAPE BOOTS

With boot colour of chosen elf, cast on 28 sts.
First row: K9, cast off next 10 sts, K to end (18 sts).
Next row: P across row, joining up gap tightly in middle.
Next row: K6, K2 tog 3 times, K to end.
Next row: P5, P2 tog 3 times, P to end.
Next row: K4, K2 tog twice, K4.
Next row: P4, P2 tog, P4.
K 2 rows.

TO SHAPE LEGS

Change to leg colour and complete as for pixie legs.
With RS together, fold boot and oversew

sole and heel seam closed. Leave top cast off sts of toes open. Sew up back leg seam. Turn RS out and, with tiny oversew sts, sew instep seam closed and carry on sewing up seam to top front of boot, pulling sts tightly as you go to curl up the toes. Stuff legs lightly as for pixies and sew on beads.

Ears for both
LEFT EAR

With pink yarn, cast on 4 sts and K 1 row.
Next row: P2 tog, P2.
Next row: K.
Next row: P2 tog, P1.
K2 tog and fasten off, leaving a long thread to sew ears to head.

RIGHT EAR

Cast on 4 sts and P 1 row.
Next row: K2, K2 tog.
Next row: P.

Accessories

Hat for pixies

With red yarn, cast on 2 sts.

First row: Inc 1, K1.

Next row: P.

Next row: Inc 1, K1, inc 1 (5 sts).

Next row: P.

Next row: Inc 1, K1, P1, K1, inc 1 (7 sts).

Next row: Cast on 11 sts, (K1, P1) across these sts and then to end of row.

Next row: Cast on 11 sts, (P1, K1) across these sts then to end of row (29 sts).*

Next row: K.

Next and every foll alt row: P.

Next K row: (K4, K2 tog) to last 5 sts, K5.

Next K row: (K3, K2 tog) to end.

Next K row: (K2, K2 tog) to end.

Next K row: (K1, K2 tog) to end.

Next K row: K2 tog to end (5 sts).

Next K row: K2 tog, K1, K2 tog (3 sts).

Next K row: K2 tog, K1 (2 sts).

Pass 1 st over the other and fasten off. With tiny oversew sts, sew up back seam of hat on RS. Attach tiny bell. Fit onto head, with back of hat almost down to back of neck, and sew on through hat rim.

Hat for elves

With hat colour of chosen elf, cast on 30 sts and work 1 row in K1, P1 rib. Starting with a K row, st st 4 rows.

Next row: K6, (K2 tog, K6) to end.

Next and every foll alt row: P.

Next K row: (K5, K2 tog) to last 6 sts, K6.

Next K row: (K4, K2 tog) to end.

Next K row: (K3, K2 tog) to end.

Next K row: (K2, K2 tog) to end.

Next K row: (K1, K2 tog) to end.

Next K row: (K2 tog) to end.

Next row: K2 tog twice.

Next K row: K2 tog and fasten off.

With RS together, sew up seam. Turn RS out, carefully teasing out tip of hat with tapestry needle. Attach tiny bell to tip of hat. Sew onto head, bend over top of hat and catch down with a couple of sts.

Collar for pixies

Work in g. st throughout.

With red yarn, cast on 3 sts and K 1 row.

Row 1: Inc 1, K to end.

Row 2: K to last st, inc 1.

Rep last 2 rows (7 sts).

Row 5: K.

Row 6: K to last 2 sts. K2 tog through back of sts.

Row 7: K2 tog, K to end.

Rep last 2 rows (3 sts).

Row 10: K.

Rep last 10 rows 4 times.

Cast off, leaving a longish thread. With tapestry needle, weave thread along top straight edge of collar. Place collar around neck and pull up thread and sts to fit. Fasten off and sew up back seam. If you have any tiny beads, a little necklace looks nice and adds to the cheerful colours.

Tunic skirt for pixies

With green yarn, cast on 7 sts and work as for collar, repeating the 10-row pattern 5 times. Ignore the stitch counts in brackets; the maximum number of sts will be 11. Cast off and fit onto pixie.

Belt for pixies

With green yarn, cast on 3 sts and g. st 32 rows or until belt fits quite tightly around top of skirt. Sew belt together at back seam. With yellow or gold yarn, sew a square of 4 sts at centre front of belt for a buckle.

Tunic skirt for elves

Using green yarn, cast on 33 sts and K 1 row.

Starting with a K row, st st 8 rows.

Next row: (K5, K2 tog) to last 5 sts, K5. Cast off.

Jacket for elves

With green yarn, cast on 34 sts and K 2 rows.

Next row: K2, P to last 2 sts, K2.

Keeping first and last 2 sts K on every row, st st 10 more rows.

RIGHT FRONT

Next row: K7, K2 tog, turn and work on these sts only for now.

Next row: K2, P to last 2 sts, K2.

Continue in st st for 10 rows, keeping border sts correct as before and ending on a P row.

Dec 1 st at end of next and foll alt row. Leave sts on a holder.

BACK

Next row: With K side facing, rejoin yarn, K2 tog, K12, K2 tog, turn and work on these sts only for now.

Next row: K2, P to last 2 sts, K2.

Keeping border sts correct, st st 10 rows, ending on a P row.

Dec 1 st at each end of next and foll alt row.
Leave sts on a holder.
Break off yarn and rejoin to last 9 sts.

LEFT FRONT

Next row: K2 tog, K to end.
Next row: K2, P to last 2 sts, K2.
Complete as for right side, reversing shoulder shaping.

COLLAR

With P side of coat facing, K to end of left front, then across sts of back and right front (22 sts).
Next row: K2, P to last 2 sts, K2.
Keeping border sts correct, starting with a K row, st st 4 rows.
P 1 row and cast off.
Sew shoulder seams and add some beads for buttons.

Belt for elves

Using belt colour of chosen elf, cast on 2 sts and K until belt measures about 10cm (4in) unstretched.
Cast off.
Use an oddment of yellow or gold yarn or thread and shape buckle with 4 small sts using the photograph (above right) as a guide.

Waistcoat for elves

Work in g. st throughout.
With colour of choice, cast on 34 sts.
Inc 1 st at each end of next and foll alt row (38 sts).
K 6 rows straight.

TO SHAPE RIGHT SIDE

Next row: K9, turn and work on these sts only for now.
Next row: K2 tog, K to end.
Next row: K.
Rep last 2 rows twice (6 sts).

TO SHAPE RIGHT FRONT EDGE

Next row: K1, K2 tog, K to end.
K 3 rows.
Rep last 4 rows, then K 1 row to end at armhole edge.

TO SHAPE RIGHT SHOULDER

Dec 1 st at beg of next and foll alt row (2 sts).
K2 tog and fasten off.

TO SHAPE BACK

Rejoin yarn at inside (armhole) edge, K20, turn and work on these sts only for now.
K2 tog at each end of next and 2 foll alt rows (14 sts).
Work 9 rows straight.

TO SHAPE BACK SHOULDERS

Dec 1 st at each end of next and foll alt row.
Cast off.

LEFT SIDE

Rejoin yarn at inside armhole edge, K2 tog on next and 2 foll alt rows (6 sts).
Complete as for first side to end of right shoulder shaping.
Join cast off sts of fronts and back at shoulder seams. Blanket stitch around edges with light brown yarn.
Sew on buttons if required.

Leprechaun

Body and head

With green yarn, cast on 27 sts.

TO SHAPE BOTTOM

Work as for Miniature Dolls to *.
Next row: P.
Change to tan-coloured yarn.
St st 10 rows, ending on a P row.

TO SHAPE SHOULDERS AND HEAD

Next row: K4, K2 tog twice, K7, K2 tog twice, K4.
Next row: P.
Next row: K4, K2 tog, K7, K2 tog, K4 (17 sts).
Change to flesh-coloured yarn. Complete head as for Miniature Dolls from ** to end.

Ears

As for Pixies and Elves.

Arms – make 2

With pink yarn, cast on 6 sts and work hands as for Miniature Dolls to *.
Change to green yarn and K 1 row.
Next row: Inc 1, K to last st, inc 1, K1.
St st 8 rows. Mark each end of last row.
Dec 1 st at each end of next and 2 foll alt rows (2 sts).
Next row: P2 tog and fasten off.

Legs – make 2

With black yarn, cast on 10 sts.
Next row: Inc in each st (20 sts).
Next row: P.
Next row: K4, K2 tog 6 times, K4.

Next row: P.
Next row: K4, K2 tog 3 times, K4.
Next row: P.
Next row: K4, K2 tog twice, K3.
Change to tan-coloured yarn.
Next row: P3, P2 tog twice, P2 (7 sts).
St st 5 rows, ending on a K row.
Change to green yarn.
Next row: P.
Next row: Inc in every st (14 sts).
St st 11 rows. Cast off.

To make up

Make up Leprechaun, including features, in same way as for Miniature Dolls.

HAIR AND BEARD

With cream yarn, sew some hair as for Pixies and Elves. For the beard, cut a long length of cream yarn and double it up. Take the thread in through back of neck and come out at chin. Keeping thread fairly loose, darn largish stitches from chin down to chest, working first along one side of face and then the other (see photograph). Fasten off when you are happy with the amount of beard. With a pin, rough up the sts a bit until they look more like hair.

Accessories

Hat

Worked in g. st throughout.

TOP

With green yarn, cast on 5 sts. Inc in every st in next and foll alt row (20 sts).
K 5 rows straight.
Next row: K1, (m1, K4) to last 3 sts, m1, K3 (25 sts).

K 2 rows and cast off.
Fold and sew up short edges to form hat.

RIM

With green yarn, cast on 50 sts and K 2 rows.
Next row: K2 tog to end.
Cast off.
Sew rim to hat with uppermost side curling up slightly (sew two short ends together and check which side curls upwards). If you find you have sewn the rim on the wrong way up, just turn the hat inside out.

HAT BAND

With black yarn, cast on 32 sts.
Cast off.
Stretch band and sew around sides of hat, joining short ends.
With gold or yellow yarn, sew 4 sts to form a square buckle.
Sew hat to head at a jaunty angle, taking sts deep in and out of head around inside edge where the rim meets the top.

Belt and jacket

As for Elves (brown yarn for belt), adding a buckle to belt as for hat.

Bow tie – optional

Cast on 6 sts and K 4 rows.
Cast off.
Tie a length of yarn around middle of rectangle, pull up tightly and knot. Tie around neck.

Boots

Sew on buckle as for hat.

Teddies

Jim

Jim is a traditional type bear. He is quite easy to make and is fully poseable with thread-jointed limbs.

HEIGHT
Approximately 30cm (12in)

MATERIALS
- 2 x 50g balls DK yarn in cream for main bear colour
- Oddments of DK yarn in light brown contrast colour for paw pads
- Oddments of DK yarn in red, yellow, dark brown and blue for scarf
- Pair of 3mm knitting needles
- Black or brown yarn or embroidery thread for nose, mouth and claws
- Tapestry/yarn needle
- Polyester stuffing
- Two 7.5mm safety eyes

Bear

All pieces are knitted with main colour yarn unless otherwise stated and worked in st st, starting with a K row.

Body
Cast on 8 sts.
First row: Inc in each st (16 sts).
Next and every foll alt row: P.
Next K row: Inc 1, (K2, inc in next 2 sts) to last 3 sts, K2, inc 1 (24 sts).
Next K row: Inc 1, (K4, inc in next 2 sts) to last 5 sts, K4, inc 1.
Next K row: Inc 1, (K6, inc in next 2 sts) to last 7 sts, K6, inc 1 (40 sts).
Next K row: Inc 1, K8, (inc in next 2 sts, K8) 3 times, inc 1.
Next K row: K11, (inc in next 2 sts, K10) twice, inc in next 2 sts, K11 (54 sts).
St st 11 rows.**
Dec 1 st at each end of next and foll alt row (50 sts).
St st 11 rows.
Inc 1 st at each end of next and foll alt row (54 sts).
St st 3 rows.

TO SHAPE SHOULDERS
Next row: Sl 1, K2 tog, K8, K2 tog twice, K24, K2 tog twice, K8, k2 tog, K1 (48 sts).
St st 3 rows.
Next row: K9, K2 tog twice, K22, K2 tog twice, K9 (44 sts).
Next row: P.
Next row: Sl 1, K2 tog, K5, K2 tog twice, K20, K2 tog twice, K5, K2 tog, K1 (38 sts).
Next row: P6, P2 tog twice, P18, P2 tog twice, P6 (34 sts).
Next row: Sl 1, K2 tog, K2, K2 tog twice, K5, K2 tog, K2, K2 tog, K5, K2 tog twice, K2, K2 tog, K1 (26 sts).
Cast off.

Head
FIRST SIDE
Cast on 13 sts.
First row: K.
Next row: Inc 1 at each end of row (15 sts).
Next row: Inc 1 at beg of row (16 sts).
Next row: Inc 1 at end of row (17 sts).
Rep last 2 rows twice (21 sts).
St st 4 rows, ending on a P row.

TO SHAPE NOSE
Next row: Cast off 4 sts at beg of row.
Next row: Dec 1 st at end of row.
Next row: Cast off 4 sts at beg of row, slipping the first st (12 sts).

Next row: Dec I st at beg of row.
Next row: K.
Dec I st at each end of next 2 rows.
Cast off remaining 7 sts, purling 2 sts together at each end of row at same time.

SECOND SIDE
Cast on 13 sts.
First row: P.
Next row: Inc I st at each end of row.
Next row: Inc I st at beg of row.
Next row: Inc I st at end of row.
Rep last 2 rows twice (21 sts).
St st 4 rows, ending on a K row.

TO SHAPE NOSE
Next row: Cast off 4 sts at beg of row.
Next row: Dec I st at end of row.
Next row: Cast off 4 sts at beg of row, slipping the first st (12 sts).
Next row: Dec I st at beg of row.
Next row: P.
Dec I st at each end of next 2 rows.
Cast off remaining 7 sts, knitting 2 sts tog at each end of row at same time.

HEAD GUSSET
Starting at back neck edge.
Cast on 2 sts.
Next row: Inc in each st (4 sts).
Next row: P.
Inc I st at each end of next and every foll 4th row until 14 sts.
St st 9 rows, ending on a P row.

TO SHAPE NOSE
Dec I st at each end of next and every alt row until 6 sts.
St st 7 rows.
Next row: K2 tog, K2, K2 tog.
Cast off.

Ears – make 4 pieces
Cast on 10 sts.
St st 4 rows.
Dec I st at each end of next 2 rows.
Cast off remaining 6 sts, knitting 2 sts tog at each end of row at same time and leaving a long tail.

Right arm
Beginning at paw, with contrast yarn, cast on 4 sts.
Inc I st at each end of next and foll alt row (8 sts).
Next row: P.
Inc I st at beg of next and foll alt row (10 sts).
Next row: P.
Next row: Inc I st at beg and dec I st at end of row.
Next row: P.
Rep last 2 rows twice.
Next row: Dec I st at end of row.*
Break yarn and leave these sts on a holder.
With main colour yarn, cast on 4 sts and inc I st at each end of next and foll alt row (8 sts).
Next row: P.
Inc I st at end of next and foll alt row (10 sts).
Next row: P.

Next row: Dec I st at beg and inc I st at end of row.
Next row: P.
Rep last 2 rows twice.
Next row: Dec I st at beg of row (9 sts).**

TO JOIN PAW PAD TO ARM
Next row: P to end of row, then across sts on holder.
Next row: K8, K2 tog, K to end (17 sts).
Next row: P.
Inc I st at each end of next and every foll 6th row until 23 sts.
St st 5 rows straight.
Next row: K2 tog, K7, K2 tog twice, K8, K2 tog.
Next row: P.
Next row: K2 tog, K5, K2 tog twice, K6, K2 tog.
Next row: P6, P2 tog, P7.
Cast off remaining 14 sts, knitting 2 sts tog at each end of row at same time.

Left arm
With main colour yarn, work as for right arm to *.
With contrast yarn for paw pad, work from * to **.
Break contrast yarn, rejoin main colour and continue from ** to end.

Legs – make 2
Cast on 30 sts.
St st 4 rows.
Dec I st at each end of next and foll alt row (26 sts).
Next row: P.

To shape foot, cast off 4 sts at beg of next 2 rows (18 sts).

St st 2 rows.

Inc 1 st at each end of next and every foll 4th row until 28 sts.

St st 5 rows.

TO SHAPE TOP OF LEG

Next row: K2 tog, K10, K2 tog twice, K10, K2 tog (24 sts).

Next row: P.

Next row: K2 tog, K8, K2 tog twice, K8, K2 tog (20 sts).

Cast off, purling 2 sts tog at each end of row at same time.

Soles – make 2

With contrast yarn, cast on 3 sts.

Inc 1 st at each end of next and every foll alt row until 9 sts.

St st 9 rows.

Dec 1 st at each end of next and foll alt row (5 sts).

Cast off, purling 2 sts tog at each end of row at same time.

To make up

Sew all pieces K sides tog.

BODY

Fold lengthways, pin and sew up from bottom to top, leaving a gap about halfway for turning and stuffing. The seam will lie at centre back of bear. Stuff firmly.

HEAD

Pin and sew two side pieces of head together from front neck to tip of nose. Pin and sew head gusset to both sides of head, starting at nose and working around to back of head, adjusting to fit and making sure both sides are even. Stuff temporarily and position eyes (see page 13). When you are happy with them, carefully remove them and place a marker where the shanks are to go. Remove the stuffing and fit the eyes securely.

Stuff carefully, filling out nose and shaping head, then sew to body all around neck edges, pushing in more stuffing before finally closing the seam.

Embroider a nose using full thickness embroidery thread. Start off with 3 long sts to make a frame and then fill in long sts either vertically or horizontally if you prefer. Shape a mouth with 3 more sts (see photograph on page 74, as a guide).

EARS

Match up the pairs of ears, pin and sew up around curved edges, leaving bottom edge open. Turn RS out, press flat and oversew closed. Sew quite well back on head and about halfway across gusset seams, pulling bottom corners of ears forwards to make a nice curve.

ARMS AND LEGS

Fold each arm lengthways, pin and sew up, leaving a small gap at back for turning and stuffing. Turn RS out and stuff carefully; check they match in size and then sew up gap in the seams. Fold each leg in half lengthways, pin and sew around top and down front, leaving a small gap for stuffing and bottom edges open. Pin, adjust and sew soles to feet. Turn RS out and stuff, shaping feet carefully and then close the seam.

With 3 strands of black or brown embroidery thread, sew 3 claws on each paw.

TO ATTACH ARMS AND LEGS

Find best position for limbs by pushing a knitting needle through limbs and body as if thread-jointing. Can he sit comfortably? Remove limbs and mark required joint positions. With a long length of yarn, doubled and knotted, sew through from one limb position to another and pull quite tightly to create 'sockets'. Sew inside of limb tops to each side of body securely, matching joint markers, taking the yarn back and forth through body after each st.

Accessories

Scarf

Worked in g. st.

With red yarn, cast on 90 sts and K in stripes of 2 rows red, 3 rows yellow, 1 row dark brown and 2 rows blue.

Cast off in blue.

To add a tassel fringe, cut 10 lengths of yarn, about 10cm (4 in) long. Fold a length in half and thread folded end onto tapestry needle. Take needle through end of scarf and draw loop through. Remove needle, pull the two ends through the loop and pull gently to secure tassel. Add 4 more tassels along first end of scarf and then repeat along other end of scarf to match. Trim to neaten.

Oscar

Oscar is basically the same bear as Jim (see page 74) but knitted in a thicker yarn to create a bigger bear. He has a slightly longer body, nose and arms, and he has a contrast muzzle and inner ears as well as paw pads.

HEIGHT
Approximately 45cm (17¾in)

MATERIALS
- 1 x 100g ball Aran yarn in medium brown for main bear colour
- Oddment of Aran yarn in oatmeal for contrast colour
- 1 x 25g ball DK yarn in yellow for waistcoat
- Oddment of DK yarn in red for waistcoat edging (optional)
- Pair of 4mm knitting needles
- Tapestry/yarn needle
- Polyester stuffing
- Two 12mm safety eyes
- 4 sets of 35mm plastic joints
- Black yarn or embroidery thread for nose, mouth and claws
- 2 press fasteners, for waistcoat
- 2 small buttons, for waistcoat

Bear

Throughout pattern, always twist the two yarns together when changing colour to prevent a gap from forming. Stay with each colour until told to change.

Head
FIRST SIDE
With brown yarn, cast on 13 sts.
Row 1: Join in contrast yarn and K first st, change to brown yarn and K to end.
Row 2: Inc 1, P to last st, change to contrast yarn and inc 1.
Row 3: Inc 1, K1, change to brown yarn and K to end.
Row 4: P to last 3 sts, change to contrast yarn, P1, inc 1, P1.
Row 5: Inc 1, K3, change to brown yarn and K to end.
Row 6: P to last 5 sts, change to contrast yarn, P3, inc 1, P1.
Row 7: Inc 1, K5, change to brown yarn and K to end.
Row 8: P to last 7 sts, change to contrast yarn, P5, inc 1, P1.
Row 9: Inc 1, K7, change to brown yarn and K to end.
Row 10: P to last 9 sts, change to contrast yarn, P7, inc 1, P1 (22 sts).

Keeping colours as set, st st 4 rows and then follow instructions for Jim from nose shaping, casting off 5 sts at beg of the two K rows instead of 4. Break contrast yarn when finished with it.

SECOND SIDE
Work as for first side, reversing colours and shaping by starting with a P row and reading P for K and K for P to end.

HEAD GUSSET
Work as for Jim until 10 sts remain when decreasing for nose, ending on a P row. Change to contrast colour yarn and complete as for Jim.

Ears – make 4 pieces
Make 2 pieces in brown and 2 in contrast colour.
Cast on 12 sts. Complete as for Jim.

Legs – make 2
Work as for Jim to top of leg shaping, but cast on 32 sts instead of 30.
Cast off 5 sts instead of 4 at beginning of two rows for foot shaping.

Inc up to 26 sts instead of 28, and finish with 11 rows st st instead of 5.

TO SHAPE TOP OF LEG
Next row: K2 tog, K9, K2 tog twice, K9, K2 tog (22 sts).
Next row: P.
Next row: K2 tog, K7, K2 tog twice, K7, K2 tog (18 sts).
Cast off, purling 2 sts tog at each end of row at same time.

Arms
As for Jim, adding four extra rows to length before shaping top.

Soles – make 2
As for Jim, working two extra rows to lengthen slightly.

Body
As for Jim, but st st 15 rows twice instead of 11 to lengthen body.

To make up
Make up Oscar as for the Jim bear. You could thread-joint the limbs as for Jim or use plastic joints as here, which I find look nicer on this larger bear. These can be found in most yarn and haberdashery shops and are quite easy to insert. Take care to match the contrast colour on the muzzle pieces when making up the head. The head is sewn to the body as for Jim.

Accessories
Waistcoat
Worked in g. st. There is no RS or WS so both fronts are the same.
FRONTS – MAKE 2
With yellow yarn, cast on 2 sts.
Inc 1 st at each end of next and every foll alt row until 20 sts.
K straight until work measures 7cm (2¾in) from cast on.

TO SHAPE ARMHOLE
Cast off 2 sts at beg of next and 2 foll alt rows (14 sts).
K 3 rows, ending at side edge.

TO SHAPE FRONT EDGE
Next row: K to last 3 sts, K2 tog, K1 (13 sts).
K 3 rows.
Cont to dec in next and every 4th row until 8 sts remain, ending at front edge.
Next row: K.

TO SHAPE SHOULDER
Next row: Cast off 2 sts, K to end (6 sts).
Next row: K.
Next row: Cast off 2 sts, K2 tog, K1 (3 sts).
Next row: K.
Cast off.

BACK
Cast on 36 sts and work straight until back measures same as side edges of fronts up to armhole shaping.

TO SHAPE ARMHOLES
Cast off 2 sts at beg of next 6 rows (24 sts).
Cont straight until back measures same as fronts to top of shoulders.

TO SHAPE SHOULDERS
Cast off 2 sts at beg of next 6 rows (12 sts).
Cast off.

POCKET
Cast on 6 sts and K 1 row.
Inc 1 st at beg and end of next and foll alt row (10 sts).
K 6 rows straight.
Cast off.
Sew up shoulder and side seams. Blanket st around outside edges with red yarn. Sew press fasteners to front edges of waistcoat and buttons to outside of waistcoat over top of fasteners (there are no button holes).
Sew on pocket as in photograph.

Duncan

This miniature bear is ideal as a collector's bear, mascot or pocket-sized friend. He is not suitable for young children because of his size and tiny bead eyes.

HEIGHT
Approximately 13cm (5in)

MATERIALS
- Oddments of 4ply yarn in colours of your choice for bear, jacket and scarf
- Pair of 2.25mm knitting needles
- Two 3mm black beads
- Black sewing thread and small sewing needle
- Tapestry/yarn needle
- Small amount of polyester stuffing
- Black or brown embroidery thread for nose, mouth and claws
- Forceps or tweezers
- 3 tiny press fasteners for jacket

Bear

All pieces are worked in st st, starting with a K row, unless otherwise stated.

Body and head
Cast on 8 sts.
Row 1: Inc in each st (16 sts).
Row 2: P.
Row 3: Inc in each st (32 sts).
St st 7 rows.
Row 11: Dec 1 st at each end of row.
St st 9 rows.
Row 21: Inc at each end of row.
St st 3 rows.
Row 25: K6, K2 tog, K6, K2 tog twice, K6, K2 tog, K6 (28 sts).
Row 26: P.
Row 27: (K2 tog, K4) twice, K2 tog twice, (K4, K2 tog) twice (22 sts).
Row 28: P.
Row 29: K2 tog, K4, K2 tog, K6, K2 tog, K4, K2 tog (18 sts).
Row 30: P2 tog, P5, P2 tog twice, P5, P2 tog (14 sts).
Row 31: K.

TO SHAPE HEAD
Row 32: Inc 1, P5, inc in next 2 sts, P5, inc 1.
Row 33: K8, inc in next 2 sts, K8.
Row 34: P9, inc in next 2 sts, P9.
Row 35: K10, inc in next 2 sts, K10.
Row 36: P11, inc in next 2 sts, P11.
Row 37: K12, inc in next 2 sts, K12 (28 sts).
Row 38: P14, turn and work on these sts only for now.

TO SHAPE ONE SIDE OF NOSE
Next row: Cast off 6 sts, K to last 2 sts, K2 tog.
Next row: P.
Next row: K2 tog, K3, K2 tog.
Cast off, slipping the first st.

TO SHAPE OTHER SIDE OF NOSE
Next row: With P side facing, rejoin yarn, cast off 6 sts, P to last 2 sts, P2 tog.
Next row: K.
Next row: P2 tog, P3, P2 tog.
Cast off, slipping the first st.

HEAD GUSSET
Beginning at nose, cast on 2 sts, leaving a long thread.
First row: Inc in each st (4 sts).
St st 5 rows.
Inc 1 st at each end of next and foll alt row (8 sts).
St st 9 rows.

Dec 1 st at each end of next and foll alt row (4 sts).
Next row: P.
Next row: K2 tog twice (2 sts).
Pass 1 st over the other and fasten off.

Ears – make 2

Worked in g. st.
Cast on 8 sts and K 3 rows.
Next row: K2 tog, K4, K2 tog.
Cast off, knitting 2 sts tog at each end of row at same time and leaving a long thread.

Arms – make 2

Starting at paw, cast on 3 sts.
Row 1: Inc in each st (6 sts).
Row 2: P.
Row 3: Inc 1, K1, inc in next 2 sts, K1, inc 1 (10 sts).
Row 4: P.
Row 5: Inc 1, K2, K2 tog twice, K2, inc 1 (10 sts).
Row 6: P.
Rep last 2 rows twice.
St st 6 rows.
Row 17: Inc 1, K to last 2 sts, inc 1, K1 (12 sts).
St st 5 rows.
Row 23: K2 tog, K2, K2 tog twice, K2, K2 tog (8 sts).
Row 24: P.
Row 25: (K2 tog, K1) twice, K2 tog.
Cast off, slipping the first st.

Legs – make 2

Cast on 20 sts.
Starting with a P row, st st 2 rows.

TO SHAPE TOES

Row 3: Dec 1 st at each end of row.
Row 4: Cast off 4 sts, K to last 4 sts, cast off 4 sts (10 sts). Break yarn.
Row 5: Rejoin yarn and P.
Inc 1 st at each end of next and every foll 4th row until 16 sts.
St st 5 rows.
Row 20: K2 tog, K4, K2 tog twice, K4, K2 tog (12 sts).
Row 21: P.
Row 22: K2 tog, K2, K2 tog twice, K2, K2 tog (8 sts).
Cast off purlwise.

Soles

Cast on 3 sts.
Row 1: Inc at each end of row (5 sts).
St st 8 rows.
Row 10: Dec 1 st at each end of row (3 sts).
Cast off, slipping the first st.

To make up

Press all pieces lightly. Sew in all loose ends except the long thread at top of ears and at nose end of gusset. Match all pieces P sides together to sew up. Use an oversew stitch and sew very small stitches close together, checking frequently that seams are still aligned. Use ladder stitch to close gaps in seams after stuffing.

HEAD AND BODY

Sew 1 or 2 sts to neaten off seam at tip of nose. With P sides together, sew head gusset to both sides of head from nose to back of neck, adjusting to fit. Join body pieces from back of neck to about 1cm

(½in) down shoulders and back, and from lower back to bottom. Turn RS out through gap and stuff carefully, filling nose first and moulding into shape as you go. Close the back opening. Tie a piece of the same colour yarn around neck and pull firmly to define neck and shoulders. Tie a knot and sink the yarn ends into body.

EARS

Sew in cast on thread. Weave long cast off thread through sts at edge of one side of ear down to base, and pull slightly to 'round off' top of ear, then take a couple of sts to anchor the thread. Pin and sew ears to head, almost at back of head and over gusset line.

EYES

Mark position of eyes with pins. Thread each bead 'eye' onto black thread, then thread both ends onto the tapestry needle. Push the needle into the eye position and then out at back of neck, pulling thread ends through. Leave them hanging for now and repeat with other bead, bringing needle and threads out at same place at back of head. Pull both sets of threads to

Insert the eyes.

embed the eyes, tie off securely, trim and sink yarn ends into head out of sight.

NOSES AND MOUTH
With 2 strands of embroidery thread, sew a small neat triangle for the nose and 2 or 3 sts for the mouth.

ARMS
With P sides together, fold and sew up arm seams, leaving a small gap for turning and stuffing at the back. Turn RS out and stuff carefully, then sew up gap.

LEGS
With P sides together, sew up back leg seam, leaving bottom edge open and a small gap for turning and stuffing. Sew in the soles. Turn RS out and stuff, then close gap. Sew 3 claws onto each paw.

TO ATTACH THE LIMBS
Pin arms and legs to body, with top of arms a little way down from top of body, and top of legs about 1cm (½in) up from teddy's bottom (check that he can sit correctly). Remove arms and legs for now, replacing pins in exact position where limb 'joints' are going to be, then attach the limbs using the thread-jointing technique (see page 13).

Accessories
Jacket
BACK AND FRONTS
Cast on 43 sts.
First row: K2, P1, (K1, P1) to last 2 sts, K2.
Next row: K3, (P1, K1), to last 2 sts, K2.

Next row: K.
Next row: K2, P to last 2 sts, K2.
Repeat last 2 rows twice.

RIGHT FRONT
Next row: K9, K2 tog, turn and work on these sts only for now.
Next row: P to last 2 sts, K2.
Next row: K to last 2 sts, K2 tog.
Next row: P to last 2 sts, K2.
Rep last 2 rows 4 times (5 sts).
Break yarn and leave sts on a holder.

BACK
With RS facing, rejoin yarn to remaining sts.
Next row: K2 tog, K17, K2 tog, turn and work on these sts only for now.
Next row: P.
Cont to dec as in last 2 rows until 9 sts remain, ending on a P row.
Break yarn and leave sts on a holder.

LEFT FRONT
With RS facing, rejoin yarn to remaining 11 sts.
Next row: K2 tog, K to end.
Next row: K2, P to end.
Rep last 2 rows 5 times (5 sts).
Leave sts on a holder.

SLEEVES – MAKE 2
Cast on 15 sts.
First row: K1, (P1, K1) to end.
Next row: P1, (K1, P1) to end.
St st 2 rows.
Inc 1 st at each end of next and foll alt row (19 sts).
St st 3 rows. Mark each end of last row.

To shape top, dec 1 st at each end of next and every foll alt row until 7 sts.
Next row: P to end and leave sts on a holder.

TO JOIN THE PIECES
Press all pieces under a damp cloth. With RS facing, sew sleeve seams from cuff to markers. Turn RS out, fit into jacket and sew up raglan seams.
With RS facing, slip sts from holders onto a knitting needle and K across them in following order: 5 sts of right front, 7 sts of right sleeve, 9 sts of back, 7 sts of left sleeve and 5 sts of left front (33 sts).
Next row: K2, (P2, P2 tog), to last 3 sts, P1, K2 (26 sts).

NECKLINE AND HOOD
Next row: Cast off 2 sts, K1, (P1, K1) to last 2 sts, K2.
Repeat last row (22 sts).
Starting with a K row and keeping first and last 2 sts K in every row (for hood border), work 12 rows st st.
Next row: K11, turn and work on these sts only for now.*
Next row: P2 tog, P to last 2 sts, K2.
Next row: K.
Cont to dec at back edge on next and every alt row until 8 sts. Cast off.
With RS facing, rejoin yarn to second side of hood.
Next row: K to end.
Next row: K2, P to last 2 sts, P2 tog.
Repeat last 2 rows until 8 sts remain.
Cast off. Sew up back hood seam from * to g. st border and rest of jacket seams.
Sew press fasteners to jacket borders.

Harriet

This little bear is very quick and easy to make. She is ideal as a toy for younger children as there are no little pieces to pull off (you can omit any beads, depending on age of child). Even her ears are slotted into her head and sewn from the inside.

HEIGHT OF BEAR
Approximately 21cm (8¼in)

LENGTH OF BED
Approximately 30cm (12in)

MATERIALS FOR BEAR
- 1 x 50g ball DK yarn in sand/fawn colour (this would be enough to make about 3 bears)
- Oddments of DK yarn in lilac, white, denim and yellow for clothes
- Oddment of pink yarn to embellish pyjamas (optional)
- Pair of 3mm knitting needles for bear
- Pair of 3.25mm kniting needles for clothes
- Brown embroidery thread
- Tapestry/yarn needle
- Small amount of polyester stuffing
- 3 medium press fasteners (1 for pyjamas, 2 for dungarees)

MATERIALS FOR BED
- 2 x 50g balls DK yarn in cerise
- 1 x 50g ball DK yarn in pale pink
- Oddment of DK yarn in white
- Pair each of 3.25mm and 4mm knitting needles
- Oddment of light blue felt
- Polyester stuffing for pillow
- A few beads to decorate (optional)

Bear

Body and legs
RIGHT LEG
With 3mm needles starting with feet, cast on 6 sts.
First row: Inc knitwise in every st (12 sts).
Next row: P.
Next row: Repeat first row (24 sts).
St st 3 rows.*
Next row: K3, K2 tog 6 times, K9.
Next row: P.
Next row: K3, K2 tog 3 times, K9.

TO SHAPE TOP OF LEG
St st 9 rows straight.
Next row: Inc 1, K to last 2 sts, inc 1, K1 (17 sts).
St st 7 rows, ending on a P row.
Mark each end of last row** and leave sts on a holder.

LEFT LEG
Work as for right leg, reversing shaping from * thus:
Next row: K9, K2 tog 6 times, K3.
Next row: P.
Next row: K9, K2 tog 3 times, K3.
Complete as for left leg from top of leg shaping to **.

TO JOIN LEGS FOR BODY
Next row: Inc 1, K to last 2 sts, inc 1, K1, join in right leg thus: inc 1, K to last 2 sts, inc 1, K1 (38 sts).
Next row: P.
Next row: Inc 1, K to last 2 sts, inc 1, K1.
Next row: P.
Next row: K10, turn, sl 1, P back.
Next row: K8, turn, sl 1, P back.
Next row: K6, turn, sl 1, P back.
Next row: K4, turn, sl 1, P back.
Next row: K2, turn, sl 1, P back.
Next row: K to end.
Next row: P10, turn, sl 1, K back.
Cont down to 2 sts as with K rows.
Next row: P to end.
St st 12 rows straight.

TO SHAPE LEFT BACK
Next row: K8, K2 tog, turn and work on these sts only for now.
Next row: P.
Next row: K to last 2 sts, K2 tog.
Cont to dec in this way at armhole edge until 4 sts remain, ending on a P row.
Cast off.

TO SHAPE FRONT

With K side facing, rejoin yarn, K2 tog, K16, K2 tog.

Next row: P.

Continue to dec at each end of K rows until 8 sts remain, ending on a P row.

Cast off.

TO SHAPE RIGHT BACK

Rejoin yarn and complete as for left back, reversing shaping.

Head

Starting at front neck, cast on 14 sts.

First row: K6, inc in next 2 sts, K6.

Next row: P.

Next row: K7, inc in next 2 sts, K7.

Next row: P.

Cont to inc in this way until you have 22 sts, ending on a P row.

St st 2 rows straight.

Next row: K9, K2 tog twice, K9.

Next row: P.

Next row: K8, K2 tog twice, K8.

Next row: P.

Mark each end of last row.

Next row: K2 tog, K5, K2 tog twice, K5, K2 tog.

Next row: P.

Next row: K2 tog, K3, K2 tog twice, K3, K2 tog.

Next row: P.

Next row: K2 tog at each end of row (8 sts).

Next row: P.

Next row: Inc 1, K to last 2 sts, inc 1, K1.

Next row: P.

Rep last 2 rows twice (14 sts).

Mark each end of last row.

St st 10 rows straight.

Dec 1 st at each end of next and foll alt row.

Next row: P.

Cast off.

Ears – make 2

Cast on 7 sts.

Starting with a P row, st st 3 rows.

K2 tog at each end of next and foll alt row (3 sts).

Next row: Inc purlwise in first 2 sts, P1.

Next row: Inc 1, K2, inc 1, K1 (7 sts).

St st 3 rows.

Cast off.

Arms – make 2

Cast on 5 sts.

First row: Inc in every st (10 sts).

Next row: P.

Next row: Inc 1, K to last 2 sts, inc 1, K1.

St st 7 rows.

Inc 1 st at each end of next and foll alt row (16 sts).

St st 3 rows. Mark each end of last row.

TO SHAPE TOP OF ARMS

Next row: K2 tog at each end of row.

Next row: P.

Rep last 2 rows until 4 sts remain.

Cast off.

To make up

Sew up all pieces with RS together unless otherwise stated.

EARS

Fold ears and sew up side seams. Turn RS out and oversew bottom edges.

HEAD

With RS together, fold head and sew side seams from neck to markers. The gaps left are for inserting the ears. Carefully fit bottom edge of ears into gaps, lining up all edges and sew firmly through all layers. Turn head RS out and stuff.

ARMS, BODY AND LEGS

Fold each arm lengthways and sew up to markers. Turn RS out.

Fold body and legs so that seam lies at back. Sew up legs, bottom and back, leaving a gap at centre back to make stuffing easier. Insert arms and sew up raglan seams.

Stuff legs and body firmly except around tops of legs and at raglan arm seams where there should be less stuffing to allow for easier movement. To further help teddy to sit, sew a small running st diagonally from crotch to hips through all layers (see diagram below).

Sew head to body, pushing more stuffing into neck as you go. Tie a length of yarn around neck, tighten slightly and sew ends into body out of sight.

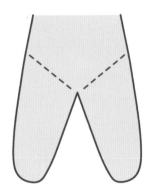

FACE

With 3 strands of brown embroidery thread, embroider the features. For sewing the eyes, you could refer to the Miniature Dolls as a guide (see page 61).

ACCESSORIES
Pyjama top
FRONT

With 3mm needles and white yarn, cast on 24 sts and work in K1, P1 rib for 2 rows.
Change to 3.25mm needles and lilac. Starting with a K row, st st 8 rows.*

TO SHAPE ARMHOLES

Cast off 2 sts at beg of next 2 rows.
K2 tog at each end of next and every alt row until 14 sts, ending on a P row.

TO SHAPE LEFT FRONT

Next row: K2 tog, K4, turn and work on these sts only for now.**
Next row: P.
Next row: K2 tog at each end of row.
Next row: P.
Next row: K2 tog, K1.
Next row: P2 tog and fasten off.

TO SHAPE RIGHT FRONT

With RS facing, leave next 2 sts on a safety pin, then K to last 2 sts, K2 tog.
Complete as for left front from **, reversing shaping.

BACK

Work as front to *.

TO SHAPE ARMHOLES AND BACK OPENING

Next row: Cast off 2 sts, K until there are 10 sts on right-hand needle, turn.
Next row: K2, P to end.
Next row: K2 tog, K to end.
Next row: K2, P to end.
Rep last 2 rows until 5 sts.
Leave sts on a safety pin.
Next row: With RS facing, rejoin yarn, cast on 2 sts at beg of row, K to end.
Next row: Cast off 2 sts, P to last 2 sts, K2.
Next row: K to last 2 sts, K2 tog.
Next row: P to last 2 sts, K2.
Rep last 2 rows until 7 sts.
Leave sts on a holder.

SLEEVES – MAKE 2

With 3mm needles and lilac yarn, cast on 18 sts and work in K1, P1, rib for 2 rows.
Change to 3.25mm needles and white.
Next row: Inc 1, K to last 2 sts, inc 1, K1.
Next row: P.

TO SHAPE TOP OF SLEEVES

Cast off 2 sts at beg of next 2 rows.
Dec 1 st at each end of next and every foll alt row until 6 sts, ending on a P row.
Leave sts on holder for now.

NECK

Sew up raglan seams.
With RS facing, 3mm needles and white yarn, K across 7 sts of left back, 6 sts of left sleeve, pick up and K 4 sts along left front, K2 from holder, pick up and K 4 sts along right front, K across 6 sts of right sleeve and 5 sts of right back (34 sts).

Rib 1 row.
Cast off in rib.
Sew up remaining underarm seams.
Neaten back opening with a couple of sts and sew on a press fastener.
With pink yarn, sew a line of running st around neck and tie in a bow at front.

Pyjama trousers – make 2 pieces

Starting at ankle, with 3mm needles and lilac yarn, cast on 26 sts and work in K1, P1 rib for 2 rows.
Change to 3.25mm needles and white yarn.
St st 14 rows, ending on a P row.

TO SHAPE CROTCH

Cast off 2 sts at beg of next 2 rows.
St st 12 rows, ending on a P row.*
Next row: K4, (K2 tog, K4) to end.
Change back to 3mm needles and work 2 rows in rib.
Cast off in rib.

TO MAKE UP

With RS together, fold each leg in half lengthways and sew up leg seam. Turn one leg RS out and fit this inside other leg. Sew up crotch seam and turn RS out. With pink yarn, sew a line of running st around bottom of each trouser leg if you wish.

Dungarees
FIRST LEG

With denim yarn, work as for pyjama trousers to *.
Leave sts on a spare needle.

SECOND LEG

Work as for first leg to *.
Next row: K to end of row and then across first 10 sts of first leg, turn and K20, turn and leave all remaining sts on a safety pin.

BACK OF BIB

Next row: K1, K2 tog, K to last 3 sts, K2 tog, K1.
Next row: K1, P to last st, K1.
Cont to dec in this way until 10 sts remain, ending on a K row.
Next row: K3, cast off next 4 sts, K to end.
You should have two sets of 3 sts each for the straps.
Working in g. st, K 20 rows for each strap and cast off.

FRONT OF BIB

With RS facing, rejoin yarn and K across sts of left and then right leg (24 sts).
Next row: K.

Next row: K1, K2 tog, K to last 3 sts, K2 tog, K1.
Next row: K1, P to last st, K1.
Cont to dec in this way until 10 sts remain, ending on a K row.
Next row: K.
Cast off.
Fold and sew up inside leg seams and then crotch seam. Sew press fasteners to ends of straps and on front bib.

POCKET

Cast on 6 sts and P 1 row.
Next row: Inc 1, K to last 2 sts, inc 1, K1.
St st 4 rows, ending on a K row.
Cast off and sew to front bib.

Roll-neck sweater
FRONT AND BACK – ALIKE

Using soft yellow yarn throughout, work as for front of pyjama top to start of armhole shaping.

TO SHAPE ARMHOLE

Cast off 2 sts at beg of next 2 rows.
Dec 1 st at each end of next and every alt row until 10 sts remain, ending on a P row. Leave sts on a holder.
Make a second piece the same.

SLEEVES – MAKE 2

With 3mm needles, cast on 18 sts and work in K1, P1, rib for 2 rows.
Change to 3.25mm needles.
St st 2 rows.
Next row: Inc 1, K to last 2 sts, inc 1, K1.
St st 3 rows.
Complete as for pyjama sleeves from top of sleeve shaping (6 sts).

NECK

With RS facing, sew up 3 of the raglan seams.
Starting at edge of remaining open seam, K across all sets of sts.
Work in K1, P1 rib for 7 rows.
Cast off in rib.
Sew up remaining seam.

Day bed

I have used 4mm needles for the bed base to speed things up a bit as it is quite a long piece before folding, but the top cover looks neater knitted with smaller 3.25mm needles.

BASE

With 4mm needles and cerise yarn, cast on 50 sts and work in st st until bed measures about 60cm (24in).
Cast off.

TOP COVER

The top cover is knitted sideways. You will need to wind off a second small ball of light pink yarn to join in and continue after

each 1 row of white and have 4 small lengths of white yarn, one for each row.
With 3.25mm needles and light pink yarn, cast on 40 sts.
Starting with a K row, st st 10 rows.
Join in white and K 1 row.
Join in second ball of pink and starting with a P row, st st 9 rows.
Continue to K 1 white row every 10th row until 4 stripes have been made.
St st 9 more rows, ending on a P row.
Break off pink and white and join in cerise. Work in g. st for 6 rows. Cast off.

WHITE TRIM

With 3.25mm needles and white yarn, cast on 40 sts.
Join in cerise yarn and K 1 row.
Break off, rejoin white yarn and st st for 9 more rows.
Cast off.

To make up
BASE

With RS together, fold in cast on edge so that bed section measures 22cm (8½in) and fold in cast off edge so that pillow section measures 8cm (3in). The cast on and cast off ends should meet. Sew up both long sides from top to bottom, leaving cast on/off edges open. Turn RS out.
Flatten around seams with your fingers and thumb. Pin down cast on/off edges. With cerise yarn, backstitch through both layers about 1.5cm (½in) in from edge all around bed.
Backstitch cast on (bed) edge to bottom of bed, leaving pillow open. Remove pins,

stuff pillow section and then oversew closed (as diagram below).

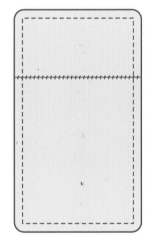

TOP COVER

Lay out top cover so that WS is facing and pink edging is on right-hand side. Stripes should be vertical. With WS of white trim facing, pin and sew cast off edge to cover, using a small backstitch.
Turn work over, fold trim forwards to right side so that most of it is showing on the front; leave about 0.5cm (¼in) at the back so you cannot see the join. Sew cast on edge to cover using small running st. Lay cover onto bed with RS uppermost. Sew right-hand side of cover to backstitch line on right-hand side (as you look at it) of bed. Sew 3 press fasteners, evenly spaced, to left side of bed and the corresponding parts to WS of cover on g. st border.

DECORATION

Decorate bed and pillow with felt hearts cut from light blue felt, using the heart templates as a guide (see page 96) , and add some beads if required. Embellish the cover trim with beads if you wish (see photograph). I have also sewn a couple of daisy sts onto the pillow.

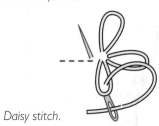

Daisy stitch.

Baby's First Teddy

These little bears are made using the Harriet bear instructions (see page 86) with a few small changes. One would make a very nice gift for a newborn baby. There are no pieces that can be pulled off, so this teddy is quite safe for young children.

HEIGHT
Approximately 18cm (7in)

MATERIALS
◆ DK baby yarn in soft pink or blue
◆ Pair of 3mm knitting needles
◆ Tapestry/yarn needle
◆ Polyester stuffing
◆ Brown embroidery thread and sewing needle
◆ Ribbon to match yarn colour

Note: I wanted to use good-quality baby yarn for these bears so had to buy 50g balls. This is far too much for one bear but the extra yarn can be saved for more bears later or passed on for someone else to make one.

Pink Bear

Work as for Harriet bear but with 2 fewer rows in first half of legs and 2 fewer rows in body before back and front shaping.

Blue Bear

This bear is also worked as for Harriet bear but with unshaped feet.

Legs and body
With blue yarn, cast on 8 sts.
Row 1: Inc in every st (16 sts).
Starting with a P row, st st 11 rows.

Next row: Inc 1, K to last 2 sts, inc 1, K1 (18 sts).
St st 7 rows.
Leave sts on spare needle and make second leg the same.

TO JOIN LEGS FOR BODY
Next row: K to last 2 sts, inc 1, K1, join in first leg thus: inc 1, K to end (38 sts).
Cont as for Harriet but work 2 fewer rows before back and front shaping.
Complete rest of bear as for Harriet.

To make up
Sew up and stuff bears following instructions for Harriet. With 2 strands of brown embroidery thread and sewing needle, embroider the features, making sure that all threads are securely fastened off because this bear will no doubt be chewed at some time. I have sewn 3 little claws on each paw but you may decide for safety to leave them off. I found some lovely pink and blue ribbon especially for new babies at a local craft shop. I should think there will be some in most yarn and haberdashery outlets.

Brian

This little chap, based on the Harriet bear (see page 86), comes already dressed.
He is so quick to knit that you could make lots of bears in different colour combinations
for children in hospital, for a fundraising event or as last-minute Christmas gifts.

HEIGHT
Approximately 20cm (7¾in)

MATERIALS
- Oddments of DK yarn in colours of your choice for bear, jumper, trousers and shoes
- Pair of 3mm knitting needles
- Tapestry/yarn needle
- Polyester stuffing
- Brown or black embroidery thread

Bear and Outfit

Arms – make 2
With bear colour, work first 5 rows as for Harriet.
Change to jumper colour.
K 1 row to form cuffs.
Starting with a K row, st st 4 rows.
Complete as for Harriet (from row 11) but leave sts on a holder instead of casting off.

Legs
With shoe colour, cast on 8 sts.
Row 1: Inc in every st (16 sts).
Starting with a P row, st st 5 rows.
Break shoe colour and join in trouser colour.
K 2 rows to form trouser hems.
Starting with a K row, st st 8 rows.
Next row: Inc 1, K to last 2 sts, inc 1, K1.
St st 7 rows.
Leave sts on spare needle and make second leg the same.
Next row: Inc 1, K to last 2 sts, inc 1, K1, join in first leg thus: inc 1, K to last 2 sts, inc 1, K1 (40 sts).
Starting with a P row, st st 7 rows.
Leave sts on spare needle.

Body
With jumper colour, cast on 40 sts. Rib 2 rows to form welt at bottom of jumper.

TO JOIN JUMPER WELT TO TROUSERS
Holding needle with jumper stitches in front of and parallel to spare needle with trouser leg sts, knit 1 st from each needle together to end.
Starting with a P row, st st 5 rows.
Complete as for Harriet from beginning of left back shaping but leave sts on a holder instead of casting off.
Sew up all raglan seams in correct order, transferring all neck sts onto one needle with RS facing (28 sts).

COLLAR
Rib 6 rows.
Cast off in rib.

Head, ears and face
As for Harriet. After stuffing, sew head to body at inside base of collar, rolling collar out of way to do so. Sew seam of jumper welt separately from body when joining back seam.

ACKNOWLEDGEMENTS

I would like to say a big thank you to the following people who gave me such help and support with this book.

To my friends and family for their encouragement and advice. Especially to my friend Carrol Bates for all the proofreading and knitting up of so many little characters and their clothes. Also for being my friend when I needed one.

Thank you also to my mother Maureen Hassell and my friend Joy Walden for their support and for patiently listening to my endless monologue of ideas, yarn colours and body shapes.

Well done Jack Hartley, my gorgeous grandson, for trying to help me knit – very good for a three-year-old but we just need a bit more practice.

There isn't too much to thank my little dog Oscar for really. Running off with the wool and trying to eat the stuffing wasn't a great deal of help.

Thank you so much to all the lovely shop owners, customers and knitters for their ideas and encouragement and for sending me their best wishes for the success of this book.

Heart template.

ABOUT THE AUTHOR

Sandra Polley has always enjoyed craftwork, especially knitting. She particularly enjoys creating little characters from scraps of yarn. Her designs have been featured in many craft and knitting magazines, such as *The Knitter*, *Simply Knitting* and *Woman's Weekly*. She also runs a successful small business, 'Knits and Pieces', selling her patterns through yarn shops and companies throughout the UK. Sandra now lives in Leicestershire and has two daughters, a young grandson and a very naughty little Border terrier called Oscar.

PAVILION

Whatever the craft, we have the book for you – just head straight to Pavilion's crafty headquarters.

Pavilioncraft.co.uk is the one-stop destination for all our fabulous craft books. Sign up for our regular newsletters and follow us on social media to receive updates on new books, competitions and interviews with our bestselling authors.

We look forward to meeting you!

www.pavilioncraft.co.uk